Waterlilies

Philip Swindells

Waterlilies

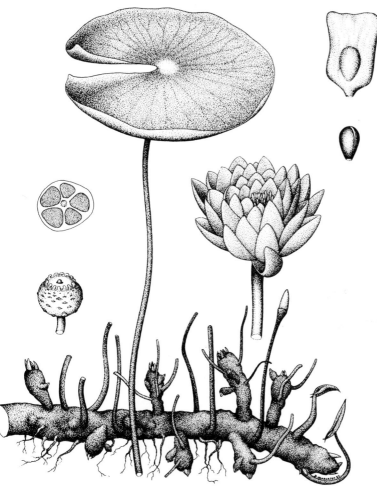

CROOM HELM London & Canberra
TIMBER PRESS   Portland, Oregon

© 1983 Philip Swindells
Croom Helm Ltd, Provident House, Burrell Row, Beckenham BR3 1AT

British Library Cataloguing in Publication Data

Swindells, Philip
   Waterlilies.
   1. Waterlilies
   I. Title
   635.93111   SB423
   ISBN 0-7099-2357-0

First published in the USA in 1983 by Timber Press,
PO Box 1631
Beaverton, OR 97075
USA
ISBN 0917304-52-7

Printed and bound in Great Britain by
Biddles Ltd, Guildford and King's Lynn

Contents

List of Figures   vii

Acknowledgements   ix

Introduction   11

  1. Waterlilies and Man   12
  2. Ecology and Botany   15
  3. Hardy Species   22
  4. Hardy Hybrids   35
  5. Tropical, Day-blooming Species   57
  6. Tropical, Night-blooming Species   66
  7. Tropical, Day-blooming Hybrids   70
  8. Tropical, Night-blooming Hybrids   81
  9. Hybridisation   87
10. Garden Pool Construction   102
11. Hardy Waterlily Culture   110
12. Tropical Waterlily Culture   123
13. Nuphars   127
14. Nelumbos   136
15. Victoria and Euryale   142
16. Pests and Diseases   145

Glossary   150

Appendix I
    The Genera *Nymphaea, Nuphar, Nelumbo, Victoria*
    and *Euryale*   152

Appendix II
    Calculating Capacities   154
    Easy Reference Table for Rectangular Pools   154
    Easy Reference Table for Circular Pools   155
    Other Useful Information   155
    Nursery Suppliers of Waterlilies   155
    Submerged Oxygenating Plants   156

Index   158

List of Figures

3.1	*Nymphaea candida*	24
3.2	*Nymphaea* 'Firecrest'	29
3.3	*Nymphaea tetragona, N. odorata* and *N. mexicana*	30
3.4	*Nymphaea tuberosa, Nuphar advena*	32
3.5	*Nymphaea tuberosa*	33
3.6	*Nymphaea tuberosa*	34
4.1	*Nymphaea* 'Amabilis'	35
4.2	*Nymphaea* 'Andreana'	36
4.3	*Nymphaea* 'Froebeli'	40
4.4	*Nymphaea* 'Gladstoniana'	40
4.5	*Nymphaea alba* and *N. marliacea* 'Carnea'	46
4.6	*Nymphaea marliacea* 'Chromatella'	46
4.7	*Nymphaea marliacea* 'Chromatella'	47
4.8	*Nymphaea marliacea* 'Chromatella', *N. marliacea* 'Carnea', *N. alba* and 'Attraction'	47
4.9	*Nymphaea* 'Mrs Richmond'	50
4.10	*Nymphaea pygmaea* 'Helvola'	53
10.1	The Basic Construction of a Concrete Pool	104
10.2	Pool Construction in Detail	106
11.1	Cutting a Square of Hessian for a Planting Basket	111
11.2	Lining the Basket with Hessian	111
11.3	Partially Filled Basket with Surplus Hessian Removed	111
11.4	Preparing the Waterlily for Planting — Removing Dead Tissue, etc.	112
11.5	Planting the Waterlily in a Heavy Loam Compost	113
11.6	Filling the Basket to Within an Inch or so of the Top	113
11.7	Covering the Basket with a Layer of Pea Shingle	113
11.8	Lowering a Basket into the Deep End	114
11.9	A Waterlily is Planted in Soil with a Layer of Gravel Above	115
11.10	Submerged Oxygenating Plants are Planted with Buried Lead Weights	115
11.12	A Well-planted Pool	117

List of Figures

11.13	A Typical Hybrid Hardy Waterlily Ready for Planting	121
13.1	*Nuphar advena, N. variegatum*	128
13.2	*Nuphar lutea*	130
13.3	*Nuphar microphylla, N. rubrodisca*	131
13.4	*Nuphar saggitifolia* and *N. polysepala*	133
14.1	Seed heads of *Nelumbo nucifera*	137
14.2	*Nelumbo nucifera*	138
14.3	*Nelumbo pentapetala*	140
15.1	Girl on a *Victoria* Leaf	143

Acknowledgements

I should like to record here my sincere thanks to the following firms and individuals who have helped me with material and advice. The co-operation extended by the staff of the Missouri Botanical Garden, St Louis, has been really wonderful, and my special thanks are extended to the Service Greenhouse Superintendent Stephen Wolff and the Librarian James Reed. Charles B. Thomas and Perry Slocum, two of America's foremost waterlily nurserymen, have also corresponded freely and given me their advice. Advice on the cultural details of *Victoria amazonica* was given by my good friend the late Len Beer, who used to grow *Victoria* to perfection when he was curator of Treborth Gardens in North Wales. The following firms have provided me with literature and information for which I am most grateful: Van Ness Water Gardens, California, William Tricker Inc., New Jersey, and Paradise Gardens Inc., Massachusetts, USA; Latour-Marliac, Temple-sur-Lot, France; Giardini di Marignolle, Florence, Italy; Liliponds (New Zealand), Napier, New Zealand; and Stapeley Water Gardens, Nantwich, Cheshire. Grateful thanks also to Mr Harold Langford who photographed many waterlilies especially for this book. Also to Stapeley Water Gardens and the editor and staff of Practical Gardening magazine for their kind assistance.

Finally, I must pay tribute to the patience of my wife and family during the undertaking of this work.

Introduction

Of all the groups of decorative plants commonly cultivated, water-lilies have been the most neglected as regards literature. Books on basic water gardening touch briefly on this gorgeous family of aquatic plants, and usually include cultural instructions and details of the more popular and easily obtainable varieties. However, nobody appears to have assembled the mass of information available into one place and presented it in a readable form. Conard's *The Waterlilies*, published in the United States in 1905, is the closest that one can come to such a work, although this is a monograph of the genus *Nymphaea* rather than a horticultural treatise, and is now outdated.

As the reader will become quickly aware, this book is not exhaustive, and in particular the descriptions of a number of the cultivars are incomplete or vague. This is partially due to the fact that some kinds were of an ephemeral nature and are in all probability extinct, although their presence here is felt necessary as they occur in horticultural literature. It can also be said that the French hybridiser Latour-Marliac should carry some of the blame, for not only did he not appear to record the parentage of his innumerable fine hybrids, but failed to make accurate descriptions of them too.

This work also embraces other genera of the Nymphaeaceae which are popularly referred to as waterlilies or pondlilies.

CHAPTER 1

Waterlilies and Man

The various genera of plants that have at different times been given the collective name of 'waterlilies', are steeped in history and tradition, particularly the *Nymphaeas* or true waterlilies.

The name *Nymphaea* is a direct transliteration of a Greek word which Theophrastus — a disciple of Plato and Aristotle — used to describe these plants some 300 years before the birth of Christ, and refers to the practice of early Greeks in dedicating the waterlily to the nymphs. This, however, is not the earliest record of the waterlily being revered, for some 1,700 years earlier the monarchy and priests of ancient Egypt were laid to rest with wreaths made from petals of the blue-flowering *Nymphaea coerulea*. The reason for this custom was the belief that the beautiful blooms of the waterlily rising pure and clean from the slimy mud, were comparable with the aspirations of man: purity and immortality.

Most of our knowledge of the history of *Nymphaeas* does in fact come from Egypt. In tombs at Beni-Hassan, a village alongside the Nile, there are pictures of gardening scenes dating from the XIIth dynasty (3000-2500 BC). One shows two gardeners bringing water from a pond to give to plants growing in square, evenly spaced beds. A narrow canal leads from the beds and terminates in the pond. It is thought that it was in this type of pond that the white-flowering *N. lotus* was often cultivated, for the ancient Egyptians at that time were using vast quantities of blooms of this species in their religious festivals, offerings of the flowers being made to the dead, or placed on altars before their gods. They were also given by the noblemen of the day to their guests as a gesture of friendship and goodwill, the visitors being expected to reciprocate by holding the blooms in their hands, or twining them in their hair whilst in the presence of their host.

Petals of *N. lotus* and *N. coerulea* were found in the funeral wreaths of Rameses II (1580 BC) and Amenhotep I; the custom being to lay wreaths on the mummy in concentric semi-circles from the chin downwards, until the sarcophagus was packed with floral tributes. Both *N. lotus* and *N. coerulea* were portrayed in the mural decorations, pottery and furniture of the period, and a little later were grown as garden plants solely for their ornamental value. Amenhotep IV grew them in ponds surrounded by flower beds in his famous palace gardens of Ikhnaton, whilst Rameses III (1225 BC) was said to grow 'rushes and the Lotus . . . and have many tanks and ponds . . . of the Lotus flowers'.

In China waterlilies are thought to have been cultivated for many years, but the ones commonly grown were the diminutive, white-flowering *N. tetragona*. Chou Tun-I, a noted author of the eleventh century, writes of the waterlily in a now much quoted passage thus:

> Since the opening days of the T'ang Dynasty it has been fashionable to admire the paeony; but my favourite is the water-lily. How stainless it rises from its slimy bed. How modestly it reposes on the clear pool, an emblem of purity and truth. Symmetrically perfect, its subtle perfume is wafted far and wide; while there it rests in spotless state, something to be regarded reverently from a distance, and not to be profaned by familiar approach.

It was believed to have been afforded similar respect by the Japanese. For their gardens invariably possessed pools, often dug out in the shape of an animal or bird, with a high bank towards the back tastefully planted with dwarfed gnarled trees overlooking spreading masses of waterlilies in the water below.

Little is known of water featuring in the gardens of the ancient Greeks until Homeric times, when they were said to have constructed nymphaeums. These were grotto-like structures surrounded by trees and with constant running water, but it is doubtful whether in fact *Nymphaeas* were grown in these situations, for they dislike both shade and moving water. The earliest reliable record of the waterlily being appreciated by the Greeks, is a mention in the first-century herbal of Dioscorides, *De Materia Medica*, and the alleged use of it symbolically in the formation of the Greek fret or meander.

In India it was seldom cultivated, but nevertheless received wide acclaim from all the great literary minds, the flower being likened to, and compared with various parts of the body. While in Britain the rootstock of *N. alba* was used more practically as a dye, in France it was an important constituent in the brewing of beer.

Although waterlilies have been cultivated in various parts of the world for many years, they are of comparatively recent introduction as garden plants in this country. The earliest reference to them seems to have been made by Phillip Miller in his *Gardeners' Dictionary* (1731): 'In some gardens I have seen plants cultivated in large troughs of water, where they flourish very well and annually produce

13

great quantities of flowers.' But few people were interested, or possibly even aware of the brightly coloured species that were being grown abroad at that time. However, Mr Paxton, gardener to the Duke of Devonshire, awakened everyone's interest in aquatic plants in 1849 by being the first person to flower a specimen of the giant waterlily *Victoria amazonica*. Two years later he added further fuel to the fire of enthusiasm for tender aquatics that was sweeping the aristocracy of the country at that time, by introducing a very fine hybrid tropical waterlily, *N.* 'Devoniensis'. Sadly, his work in the field of hybridising was not followed up until 1912, when Missouri Botanical Gardens embarked upon an extensive breeding programme. Under the very able direction of George Pring success has been swift, and now there is a truly marvellous selection of varieties in every shape, size and colour imaginable.

Similarly in the field of hardy types, the work fell almost entirely upon the shoulders of one man, Joseph Bory Latour-Marliac. In 1858 he was aroused by an article written by the celebrated botanist Leveque, who expressed deep disappointment that the bright colours and shapes of the tropical species did not exist in any of the hardy forms. At this time only the white-flowering *N. alba* was commonly grown outside, but Marliac decided that it should not be impossible to obtain coloured hardy varieties by judicious cross pollination of this with various coloured tropical species. So, with this in mind, he started to collect different species from all over the world and embarked upon a breeding programme.

For several years he worked hard, producing and flowering hundreds of seedlings with little success, until 1879 when *N. marliacea* 'Rosea' was evolved. Having obviously discovered the technique of successfully hybridising hardy *Nymphaeas*, a secret which he took with him to his grave in 1911, he produced new varieties thick and fast, and crosses raised by him were being introduced right up until 1937. Over seventy varieties were developed by Marliac, and of these only three, *N.* 'Fulva', *N.* 'Chrysantha' and *N.* 'Rosita', could be considered to be commercial failures. All the others were huge successes, and will remain a lasting tribute to one of the greatest and most gifted men ornamental horticulture has ever known.

Several other men, notably Dreer, Richardson, Perry and Buggele, can be given a certain amount of credit for having introduced one or two outstanding varieties, but in the majority of cases their successes would appear to be rather a matter of luck than good judgement.

CHAPTER 2

Ecology and Botany

The waterlily family, Nympnaeaceae, is very old and primitive and embraces nine genera: *Nymphaea, Nuphar, Nelumbo, Brasenia, Cabomba, Victoria, Barclaya, Ondinea* and *Euryale*. All members of the family have a long fossil history, rhizomes, fruits, seeds, leaves and pollen grains having been discovered in ancient rock formations. Pollen grains from what are believed to have been tropical *Nymphaeas* have been discovered in samples of coal laid down in Jurassic times, while the sacred lotus or *Nelumbo* has been recognised in the upper Cretaceous rocks of North America, Greenland and Europe. The non-European *Brasenia*, or an allied and now extinct form, is recorded from older Cretaceous rocks in Portugal, while plant remains of both *Nymphaea* and *Nuphar* are known to exist quite extensively in beds of the Tertiary age.

In fact, before the Ice Age members of the Nymphaeaceae, particularly *Nymphaeas*, were known to be widespread from the Arctic to what is now Australasia. Fossil evidence suggests that many are still in the very same form that they were over 160 million years ago, having altered only their distribution in response to climatic changes. A living example of this is the tropical species *Nymphaea lotus* which enjoys a natural distribution that extends from Egypt in the north through Central and Western Africa to Madagascar in the south, but also occurs in identical form in thermal springs in Hungary. It is believed that as the climate of Europe altered and became cooler, the populations of *N. lotus* were pushed back to North Africa, yet a small group remained in the relative warmth of the thermal springs where they have survived until the present day. This theory is reinforced by the fact that snails closely allied to those which are found in the natural habitat of *N. lotus* in Egypt are peculiar to these thermal springs too.

From this we can see that although the habit of growth and blossoms of waterlilies seem quite sophisticated, they are in fact very old plants and are well down the evolutionary scale, being in company with other garden plants like *Berberis*, *Paeonia* and *Ranunculus* in a group known botanically as the Ranales.

The *Nymphaeas* are exclusively herbaceous aquatic plants with either submerged or floating leaves, or both. They normally inhabit still, fresh water in pools and lakes, and occur in forms that will tolerate a wide range of depths. In some cases where the pool dries up for a period of time during the summer, certain species are capable of becoming dormant and resting in the form of a rhizome or tuber, while others will produce an almost terrestrial form with leaves on short petioles which lie flat on damp ground. Adaptation to this latter mode of existence is particularly noticeable with temperate species such as *N. alba* which may be temporarily aground if growing close to the edge of a pool with a variable water level. The ability to transform to a terrestial mode of life takes place quickly and without much apparent deterioration of the plant.

Most *Nymphaeas* prefer water that is neutral or slightly alkaline, few tolerating acid conditions and becoming weak and sickly when obliged to do so. In addition, waterlilies will only be discovered growing in water in an open situation with full exposure to the sun. However, in open areas subject to considerable wind and subsequent water turbulence *Nuphars* will appear where it might be thought that *Nymphaeas* would grow.

The botanical structure of *Nymphaeas* is interesting, not only because they are large and beautiful, but because they inhabit a watery environment. This adaptation to a permanent life in water, or perhaps we should more correctly say a lack of ability to evolve a terrestial habit, leads to characteristics far removed from those of their land-dwelling cousins. These are most pronounced in the foliage, which although for the most part supported by the water, suffers for this support when it comes to performing its natural functions.

Actually there are three kinds of leaves produced at various times by *Nymphaeas*: the submerged leaves, which are evident at the commencement of growth each spring and following the germination of seedlings; aerial leaves, which are peculiar to a few tropical species and which occur in other kinds when growing in overcrowded conditions; and of course the abundant and familiar floating foliage or 'lily pads', which are of the utmost importance to all species. All three kinds of leaf are generally short-lived, and are replaced regularly throughout the growing season.

Floating foliage occurs in a wide variety of shapes and sizes, leaf diameters varying from as little as 1½ in (3.8 cm) in *N. tetragona* to 2 ft (60 cm) or more in *N. gigantea* and a number of tropical cultivars. The shape of the foliage varies considerably from one species to another and may be ovate, obovate or even sagittate, although orbicular and peltate leaves are most common. However, it is typical of most species and cultivars that their leaves are cleft almost to the

16

centre where the leaf stalk or petiole is attached.

Floating leaves of no matter what shape or size are of the same construction. That is to say they have the same mathematically precise vein structure to aid their support, and an upper surface of leathery glossiness which is completely water repellant. This latter is a contrast to the underside, which is continually wet and has a strong attraction to the water. I am not qualified to explain this curious phenomenon, but it is evident to any gardener who attempts to lift an established floating waterlily leaf that there is some kind of suction, possibly surface tension, which holds the leaf to the water surface. This does not seem to be explained by the slightly downward curving leaf margins of some varieties, for in both toothed leaves and those with upturned margins the phenomenon is the same.

The upper surfaces of the leaves possess stomata as they are in direct contact with the air, but in some species stomata with large openings have been detected on the undersides where they are in continuous contact with the water. The undersides are often coloured, particularly with a bluish or violet infusion. This is anthocyanine — the normal pigment of blue flowers — and has developed in the leaf to restrict the passage of light through the normal green chlorophyll into the water beneath. By acting as a barrier this is thought to aid the processes within the leaf.

Apart from photosynthesis, which is the principal function of all green leaves, some species of tropical *Nymphaea* reproduce viviparously from their leaf sinus. The method by which this can be exploited is described in a later chapter. What actually happens is that occasionally on mature leaves a small swelling develops more or less where the leaf stalk joins the leaf. This eventually erupts and a tiny version of the parent plant develops with a cluster of leaves uppermost and often a small tuber and roots beneath. While the adult leaf remains in good condition and functions properly, the plantlet remains small and makes no significant growth. However, if the leaf starts to decay or become detached then the plantlet springs into life and starts an independent existence.

The leaves of all waterlilies are held individually on long petioles. These vary in thickness and size according to the species, but all move freely in the water and are capable of extending to allow the leaf to reach the surface should it suddenly become submerged. That is not to say that they would extend by a foot or so if their habitat were temporarily increased by that depth of water, but they are capable of fairly rapid growth which would enable a floating leaf to raise itself a few inches within a day or two. Of course, the petioles are growing steadily all the time in order to push their leaves to the outer perimeter of the plant and thus allow fresh growth to find a place in the centre.

Waterlilies have no stems as we commonly understand them, the petioles arising from tubers or rhizomes, the latter and, in some cases the former, technically being modified stems. Those species with rhizomes exhibit a circular kind of growth as the rhizomes extend and branch and the older portions die out. The tuberous-rooted kinds produce a continuous supply of young tubers which the gardener can keep each autumn for overwintering purposes (see page 125). Rhizomes and tubers of various species and cultivar groups vary considerably in size and form, and really do not merit discussion here as their particular characteristics are described under the respective species or cultivar heading.

The blossoms of *Nymphaeas* are extremely variable in shape, size and colour. There are rounded, almost ball-shaped blooms, stellate or star-shaped kinds and open plate-like blossoms as well as innumerable shapes between. Colouration is varied, and starts at a pure, glistening white passing through innumerable shades to deep purplish-black. Tropical species and cultivars embrace the whole spectrum, but blue and colour derivatives of blue are absent in the hardy kinds. However, there are interesting shades in this latter group, many of which vary from day to day as the individual blossom ages. Some cultivars pass from a clear yellow through pinks and oranges to a deep red, and are generally referred to as chameleon varieties.

The structure of *Nymphaea* blossoms varies little, but can be illustrated quite simply by the common white waterlily, *N. alba*, for in this typical member of the family the gradual stages of transformation from the green sepals of the calyx to the yellow pollen-bearing stamens can be seen clearly. If a blossom of *N. alba* can be secured and the various components separated, it will be seen that the first will be of a dark-green colouring and a definite sepal, while the next, although a paler green, is probably a sepal too, (although the botanists actually credit *Nymphaea* with but four sepals). The third graduation is neither a decided green nor a pure white but a mixture of the two, and might be called a sepal or a petal. Petals clearly follow, but in succeeding rows grade into broad, white organs which are yellow and thick at the apex with the appearance of rudimentary anther lobes. Stamens become more clearly defined towards the centre with normally developed anthers and an abundance of pollen. The transition is not in reality quite so abrupt as I have just described, for large numbers of petaloid sepals and staminiferous petals find their place between the main structural types and each differs slightly from the next.

Most species and cultivars of *Nymphaea* have a fragrance of some sort. In many of the gorgeous large-flowered cultivars it is barely perceptible, while in others it may be overpowering and sickly and

18

somewhat reminiscent of sweet violets or fresh tea. However, the value of this fragrance to the plant is questionable, for although a number rely heavily upon insects doubtless attracted by strong scents, it is also a fact that many are seldom visited by insect pollinators, and are thought by botanists to be self-pollinated. The actual process of pollination and seed production is described later in the book (see page 89) in the context in which it affects the gardener and potential hybridiser.

The genus *Nymphaea* is divided into two groups and five sub-groups. The two main groups are formed on the basis of the division of their seedpods and are called Apocarpiae and Syncarpiae respectively. The Apocarpiae are all tropical diurnal species with large fragrant blossoms held well above the water and immense leaves often with wavy or crimpled margins. Botanists further divide the Apocarpiae into two sub-groups, the Anecphya and Brachyceras, the main characteristic of members of the former group being a total lack of carpellary styles. The presence of prominent triangular, almost pyramidal, carpellary styles typifies species belonging to the Brachyceras.

The Syncarpiae embraces all the hardy species and a number of tropical kinds and is itself divided into three sub-groups; Castalia, Lotos and Hydrocallis. Castalia is the group containing all the hardy varieties and some diurnal tropicals, and is characterised by floating blossoms with short anthers and petaloid stamens. Purists have further sub-divided the sub-group into the Xanthantha for the tropical species and the Chamaenymphaea for the hardy kinds.

The groups Lotos and Hydrocallis are both tropical, the former containing all nocturnal-blooming species and the latter mostly night-flowering kinds too. Principal characteristics of the Lotos are large, strap-shaped carpellary styles and linear stamens with rounded apices. The foliage has conspicuous venation and usually sharply toothed edges as well. In most cases the flowers are held well clear of the water on strong peduncles. Conversely, the blossoms of the Hydrocallis float on the surface of the water, and can be further distinguished by large club-shaped styles and later by the distinctive hairs attached to their seeds.

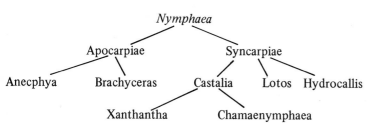

Classification of the Nymphaeas

Ecology and Botany

The *Nuphars* differ in many ways from the *Nymphaeas*, these differences being very obvious to the gardener, particularly in relation to plant habit and size of blossom. The botanist, however, does not trust such characteristics implicitly and instead makes positive identification from the foliage, in which the veins are arranged pinnately from the mid-rib, and the blossoms, in which petals and stamens are attached below the ovary. *Nuphars* all have stout creeping rhizomes which root strongly to the pool floor, translucent submerged leaves and, in most cases, stout, floating or erect foliage too. The flowers are usually held above the water and consist of between five and twelve sepals and numerous petals and stamens which grade into one another. The blossoms usually have a sickly alcoholic aroma and yield fruits that ripen above the water.

Nelumbos are quite obviously members of the Nymphaeaceae, but at the same time differ quite markedly from the rest of the family. Except in the juvenile form, their foliage remains clear of the water, borne aloft on stout, centrally placed leaf stalks which are themselves over-topped by immense blossoms. These consist of four or five sepals and myriad petals and stamens. Like *Nuphars*, *Nelumbos* grow from a stout, creeping rootstock from which the cultivars can be increased, but the species can be grown from the hard nut-like seeds which are produced in the distinctive flat-topped fruits.

Prickly foliage is one of the main characteristics of *Victoria*, although its immense size is a very obvious feature to layman and botanist alike. Huge circular leaves, from 3 to 10 feet (1 to 3 m) across, with upturned edges and reddish undersides are like nothing else in the plant kingdom. Huge fragrant blossoms comprising fifty or more oblong or narrowly obtuse petals and numerous stamens are followed by large prickly berry-like fruits. *Victoria* is a perennial with a large erect rhizome, but is usually treated as an annual when cultivated under glass in temperate regions.

Euryale is very closely allied to *Victoria*. Indeed, the latter was once placed within that genus. Some authorities believe that the two genera are so intricately bound up with one another and sufficiently different from the other members of the Nymphaeaceae that they should be hived off and placed in a new family; the Euryalaceae. At present this has not received widespread acceptance and, for the time being both *Victoria* and *Euryale* remain within the waterlily family. As intimated at the outset, both genera are closely allied, the main difference being in the slightly smaller foliage of *Euryale*, which is flat and does not have upturned edges. Petals are fewer than in *Victoria*, and these are followed by farinaceous seeds about the size of a pea.

Brasenia, like *Euryale*, is a monotypic genus comprising a solitary species with slender, creeping rootstocks which give rise to branched, leafy stems. The foliage is peltate, oval or elliptical, floating and mucilaginous on the undersurface. The blossoms are axillary and comprise three or four sepals, a similar number of petals, and up to eighteen stamens. Carpels are between four and twenty, free, and each forming a single or double-seeded nutlet which ultimately breaks open by a lid.

Here is a simple key to the identification of the genera of the Nymphaeaceae described in this work:

1. Leaves simple, entire to dentate.
2. Sinus of leaf deep, reaching almost or entirely to the petiole → 3.
   Sinus lacking; leaves centrally peltate → 4.
3. Veins mostly radiating from the petiole; petals and stamens attached on sides of ovary: *Nymphaea*.
   Veins pinnate from the midrib; petals and stamens attached below ovary: *Nuphar*.
4. Plants very prickly → 5.
   Plants not prickly → 6.
5. Plants very prickly; leaves large with upturned margins: *Victoria*.
   Plants very prickly; leaves smaller and flat: *Euryale*.
6. Leaf orbicular, 1-3 ft (30 cm-1 m) across, usually standing above the water: *Nelumbo*.

CHAPTER 3

Hardy Species

Even though there are relatively few hardy species of *Nymphaea* worthy of cultivation, the plant breeders who have worked with waterlilies have produced a wealth of outstanding cultivars for all depths of water and in almost every colour imaginable.

All hardy *Nymphaeas* bloom during the day, opening at about noon and closing as the sun goes down. Individual flowers last for up to five consecutive days in warm, sunny weather, but become water-logged or 'balled' and fail to re-open if subject to persistent rain.

Many varieties make excellent cut flowers if removed from the plants with 2 or 3 in (5-8 cm) of stem and floated on a bowl of water. The best kinds for this purpose are those with flowers that stand well clear of the water, such as *N. odorata* 'William B. Shaw' and 'Eugene de Land'. An attractive arrangement can be made with cut leaves and flowers inserted in a floral wire holder that is completely submerged in a bowl of water.

The species listed here, and the hybrids listed in Chapter 4, are arranged in alphabetical order, as their botanical affinities are often unknown. However, in some cases hybrids known to have been directly derived from a species will be found listed under that species. The natural distribution of each species is given, and in the case of hybrids, the raiser and the date of introduction, where known. The figures in parentheses following a description refer to the depths of water in which that variety is most successfully grown.

Nymphaea acutiloba See *N. tetragona*.
Nymphaea aesopii See *N. alba*.
Nymphaea alba, *Castalia alba*, *Castalia speciosa*, White Waterlily.
This is a handsome plant with snow-white, cup-shaped blossoms floating amongst orbicular, fresh, green leaves. Upon opening the flowers are fragrant, but this passes after the first day. As the flowers are visited by few insects it is thought likely that they are self-pollinated. The petals are broad and ovate, while the sepals are lanceolate, greenish-brown with white interiors. The stamens are yellow, and the fruits are generally obovoid but sometimes

globose. The rhizome is horizontal and extensive, rooting strongly along its length. A very attractive waterlily, but usually considered to be too large for the average garden pool. It was once claimed that the flowers of this species if added to distilled water would remove freckles, while a syrup compound from the petals has soothing properties. There are two clearly defined sub-species acknowledged by botanists. Europe, Africa, North and Central Asia. (Up to 10 ft (3 m)). (Fig. 4.5).

N. alba subsp. *alba* This plant is larger in every part and usually produces ovoid fruits. Europe (including British Isles). (Up to 10 ft (3 m)).

N. alba subsp. *occidentalis*, *N. alba* var. *minor*, *N. occidentalis*, Lesser White Waterlily. This is a smaller plant with fewer stigmatic rays and distinctive globose fruits. Scotland, Ireland, Hebrides, W. Norway, Denmark. (Up to 4 ft (1 m 25 cm)).

N. alba var. *maxima* This very large-flowered form is said to have originated in Macedonia. (Up to 10 ft (3 m)).

N. alba var. *minor* See *N. alba* subsp. *occidentalis*.

N. alba var. *plenissima*, *N.* 'Plenissima'. This large, double variant is thought by some to be a hybrid but is clearly not. (2-6 ft (60-90 cm)).

N. alba var. *rosea* See *N. alba* var. *rubra*.

N. alba var. *rubra*, *N. sphaerocarpa*, *N. sphaerocarpa rosea*, *N. alba* var. *rosea*, *N. caspary* Swedish Red Waterlily. This red variety is known only from lakes and ponds in Nerike in Sweden. It is seldom encountered in cultivation, but once played a prominent part in the hybridisation programme of Latour-Marliac, infusing the hitherto unknown red colouring into his hybrids. It is almost identical to the typical *N. alba*, but with flowers that open pale pink and change with age to deep plum. (Up to 10 ft (3 m)).

N. alba candidissima See *N.* 'Candidissima'.

N. alba delicata See *N.* 'Delicata'.

N. alba froebeli See *N.* 'Froebeli'.

N. alba oligostigma See *N. candida*.

N. alba oocarpa See *N. candida*.

The following specific names were given by Hentze to variants of *N. alba*, but all grade into the species. They are seldom used now, but do appear in older literature and can cause confusion.

N. aesopii This is a very large form, and is possibly *N. alba* var. *maxima*.

N. dioscoridis This small compact form is doubtless the same as, or close to, *N. alba* subsp. *occidentalis*.

N. erythrocarpa This has fruits with red internal tissue.

N. parviflora This has smaller blooms but normal size leaves.

N. splendens The flower has distinctive orange-yellow stamens.

N. urceolata This variant has an urn-shaped stigma and an increased number of petals and stamens.

N. venusta The specific characteristics of this variant are unknown.

N. biradiata See *N. candida* var. *biradiata*.

N. blanda See *N. tuberosa*.

N. candida, N. alba oocarpa, N. alba oligostigma, N. semiaperta, N. intermedia, N. punctata This is a tough, resilient species for shallow water. It has handsome, smallish, white cup-shaped blooms with golden stamens and crimson stigmas and is scentless. The sepals are ovate and tinged with green. It differs from *N. alba* in the absence of stamens on the ovary. Also the leaves have basal lobes which overlap and prominent veins on their undersides. The petioles are cylindrical and glossy; the rhizomes are erect, a couple of inches (about 5 cm) in diameter, and root strongly. N. Europe, Asia. (1-1½ ft (30-45 cm)).

Figure 3.1
Nymphaea candida

24

N. candida var. *biradiata*, *N. biradiata* A deep-red, star shape on the stigma in the centre of each bloom is the principal characteristic of this variant. The mark is composed of numerous minute purplish glands on the surface of the lower portion of the stigmatic rays, the upper portion being deep orange. (1-1½ ft (30-45 cm)).

N. candida var. *minor* This is a compact and more diminutive form. (1 ft (30 cm)).

N. candida var. *neglecta*, *N. neglecta* The petals are longer than the calyx, and the ovary is not so prominently exposed. (1-1½ ft (30-45 cm)).

N. candida var. *wanio* This is referred to in the literature, but its characteristics seem unknown. It is possibly just a fanciful botanical name.

N. candida var. *wenzelii*, *N. wenzelii* This unusual stellate form was once thought to be a distinct species. Russia. (1-1½ ft (30-45 cm)).

N. caroliniana, *N. odorata* var. *superba* This has very fragrant, soft, pink blooms with slender petals and conspicuous yellow stamens. The leaves are pale green. It is a little shy in flowering for the first year after planting. It is thought by many authorities to be a natural hybrid between *N. odorata* var. *rosea* and *N. tuberosa*. N. America. (1-1½ ft (30-45 cm)).

N. caroliniana 'Nivea' This produces large, pure-white, fragrant blooms with bright-yellow stamens. The foliage is plain green. Marliac, 1893. (1-1½ ft (30-45 cm)).

N. caroliniana 'Perfecta' This beautiful hybrid has large, fragrant, salmon-pink blossoms. Marliac, 1893. (1-1½ ft (30-45 cm)).

N. caroliniana 'Rosea' This cultivar is identical in shape and form to the species, but an agreeable shade of rose-pink. Marliac, 1908. (1-1½ ft (30-45 cm)).

N. caspary See *N. alba* var. *rubra*.

N. constans Although undoubtedly not entitled to specific rank, a pink-flowered waterlily under this name was being cultivated earlier this century. It was similar in habit to *N. odorata* var. *rosea*, and may even be a selected form of that or a hybrid made with it. It now would appear to be lost to cultivation. (1½-2 ft (45-60 cm)).

N. dioscoridis See *N. alba*.

N. erythrocarpa See *N. alba*.

N. fennica This seldom grown dwarf species has white, almost stellate, flowers and soft green leaves. The petals incurve at the tips and are often flushed pink. The rhizome is erect, 3 or 4 in (8-10 cm) long, and smothered in black root hairs. It is said by some to be a geographical form of *N. tetragona*. It requires shallow water in a cool, partially shaded position. Finland.

(1 ft (30 cm)).

N. intermedia See *N. candida.*

N. leibergii See *N. tetragona.*

N. lutea See *Nuphar lutea.*

N. maculata See *N. tuberosa.*

N. neglecta See *N. candida* var. *neglecta.*

N. nitida This unusual, small-growing species was introduced from Siberia about 150 years ago. The small, white, scentless flowers are cup-shaped and the petals blunt. The leaves are more-or-less rounded with obtuse lobes. It is suitable only for a tub or small pool. E. Europe. (1 ft (30 cm)).

N. occidentalis See *N. alba* subsp. *occidentalis.*

N. odorata, Sweet Scented Waterlily, Water Nymph. This is an excellent species for the small or medium-sized pool. Fragrant white flowers up to 6 in (15 cm) in diameter float on the surface of the water, or are occasionally held aloft. The petals are numerous, elliptical, mostly pointed, and grade through intermediate stages to stamens. There are four sepals, green on the outside but sometimes purple or maroon within. The handsome, pea-green leaves are purplish when young, and usually remain so beneath. *N. odorata* and all its varieties and hybrids have very distinctive circular leaves. The rhizomes are horizontal, thick and often very long, rooting strongly along their length. The fruit is globose, ripening beneath the water and often smothered in the decaying remains of the petals. N. America. 1786. (1½-2½ ft (45-75 cm)).

N. odorata var. *alba* This name is frequently used by nurserymen to describe *N. odorata.* However, some botanists sub-divide *N. odorata* into *N. odorata* var. *odorata* and *N. odorata* var. *alba.* The former are those plants with a pinkish flush to the petals, while the latter is appended to plants with pure-white blossoms. (1½-2½ ft (45-75 cm)).

N. odorata var. *gigantea*, *N. odorata* var. *hopatcong*, Ricefield Waterlily. This is a form with large, pure-white, incurving blossoms which are almost scentless. The leaves are huge, up to 15 in (38 cm) across, deep green and often with upturned or undulate margins. It requires plenty of room and is generally unsuitable for the garden pool. S.E. USA, Cuba, Mexico. (2-6 ft (60-90 cm)).

N. odorata var. *hopatcong* See *N. odorata* var. *gigantea.*

N. odorata var. *minor*, Mill Pond Lily. This splendid miniature variety is found in the shallow bogs of New Jersey. The extremely fragrant, star-shaped blossoms are about 3 in (8 cm) in diameter. The sepals are pale green or olive and the flower stalks mahogany in colour. The soft, green leaves are 3 to 4 in (8 to 10 cm) across with dark-red undersides. It is ideal for tubs or very shallow pools. N. America. 1812. (1 ft (30 cm)).

N. odorata var. *minor floribus roseis* This is a very choice form with soft pink reverses to the petals. It is rare in cultivation. N. America. (1 ft (30 cm)).

N. odorata var. *minor rosea* This is a strange, little, pink-flowered form whose seeds yield white-flowering progeny, and is very scarce. N. America. (1 ft (30 cm)).

N. odorata var. *odorata* This name is given by some botanists to forms of *N. odorata* with flowers lightly flushed with pink. (1½-2½ ft (45-75 cm)).

N. odorata var. *pumila* This is considered by many to be synonymous with *N. odorata* var. *minor*, but plants I have received under this name from Marliac are much different. The flowers are small, white and fragrant, while the leaves are dark-green with a purplish sheen above and deep-purple beneath. (1 ft (30 cm)).

N. odorata var. *rosea*, Cape Cod Waterlily, Boston Lily. Award of Merit 1895. First Class Certificate 1898. This soft-pink form was discovered in a low-lying valley in the Eastern United States where the plough annually unearthed large quantities of small whitish tubers. Local inhabitants, having no idea what these were, planted them, and were astonished to discover that they grew into beautiful pink waterlilies. Millspaugh introduced some into cultivation, and it is from his original plants that the commercial stocks of today were derived. It is interesting to note at this point that *N. odorata* and its varieties are capable of growing and flowering in dry conditions such as those left by the receding waters of a pond, and will survive until the rain makes good the deficit. The blossoms are 4 in (10 cm) or more across, deep pink with yellow stamens. The sepals are curious in that they remain spread open after the flower has closed. It is sweetly fragrant and seeds freely. The foliage is green, but entirely bronze in its juvenile state. It is an excellent plant for small and medium-sized pools. (1½-2 ft (45-60 cm)).

N. odorata var. *rosea* 'Prolifera' This is an improved and very free-flowering seedling. The fragrant, soft-pink flowers pass through rose to deep claret. Perry, 1900. (1½-2 ft (45-60 cm)).

N. odorata var. *rubra* This vivid crimson sport from *N. odorata* var. *rosea* was introduced into cultivation by Sturtevant in 1901. The flowers grow up to 8 in (20 cm) across and have a central boss of deep-red stamens. (1½-2½ ft (45-75 cm)).

N. odorata forma *rubra* This plant was collected from Ethel Lake, Missouri, in September 1954. Similar to *N. odorata* var. *rosea*, it was said to have been introduced to the area in the late 1940s. (1½-2 ft (45-60 cm)).

N. odorata var. *superba* See *N. caroliniana*.

N. odorata boracea An acknowledged mis-spelling of *N. odorata rosacea* occurring in the literature.

N. odorata caroliniana (*N. odorata* var. *rosea* × *N. candidissima*? or *N. tuberosa* X *N. candidissima*?) This was allegedly a plant with fragrant, salmon-pink flowers introduced in the early 1890s by Dr Henry Bahnson of North Carolina, although it appears to have been lost to cultivation now. The petals are very narrow and the stamens golden; the leaves 1 ft (30 cm) or more across, rich green above, reddish beneath and with overlapping lobes. It is said to be a parent of many modern hybrids. (1½-2½ ft (45-75 cm)).

N. odorata caroliniana nivea This is a pure white selection with fully double flowers. (1½-2½ ft (45-75 cm)).

N. odorata perfecta This is a semi-double, flesh-pink form with petals that have rounded tips. (1½-2½ ft (45-75 cm)).

N. odorata salmonea Deep salmon pink. (1½-2½ ft (45-75 cm)).

Most of these forms appear to be lost to cultivation.

N. odorata rosacea This is a hybrid form, possibly natural, with rosy-pink flowers fading to peach or yellow towards the centre. The petals are narrow and acutely pointed and the stamens bright yellow. The medium-sized foliage is plain green. (1½-2½ ft (45-75 cm)).

Hybrids derived from *Nymphaea odorata*

All the hybrids listed below are derived from *N. odorata* and retain the principal characteristics of that species. Other varieties which may contain some of this species in their make-up, but which do not retain principal characteristics, will be found under the section devoted to hybrids of unknown or mixed parentage.

'Buggele' See *N. odorata* 'Roswitha'.

'Constans' See *N. constans*.

'Eugene de Land' This bears exquisite stellate blooms of deep, glowing apricot-pink held well above the water. The petals are long and somewhat incurved, and the stamens are a deep, golden-yellow. It is richly fragrant. Marliac. (1½-2½ ft (45-75 cm)).

'Exquisita' This small-growing variety has rosy-pink stellate flowers, requires a good summer before doing well, and for this reason is more popular in warmer climates. (1 ft (30 cm)).

'Firecrest' This hybrid has striking purplish leaves and deep-pink flowers with curious, red-tipped stamens. It is American in origin. (1½-3 ft (45-90 cm)).

'Helen Fowler' The enormous, heavily scented, deep-rose flowers of this hybrid are some 10 in (25 cm) across, and are held well above the restrained, handsome, soft-green leaves. Shaw. (1½-3 ft (45-90 cm)).

'Jessieana' This bears large flowers of deep shell-pink. (1½-2 ft (45-60 cm)).

28

Figure 3.2
Nymphaea
'Firecrest'

'Luciana' This is very similar to *N. odorata* 'Exquisita', and has fragrant, deep rose-pink blossoms. For the first season the flowers float on the water, but in succeeding years are held aloft. The foliage is mid-green. Dreer. (1½-2 ft (45-60 cm)).

'Maxima' This is a large selected form of *N. odorata*. The pure-white, fragrant flowers are produced in abundance. (1½-2 ft (45-60 cm)).

'Roswitha' This popular European variety has deep, rosy-red blooms. Buggele. (1½-2 ft (45-60 cm)).

'Suavissima' The very fragrant, bright rose-pink flowers are held above the luxuriant, fresh-green foliage. The scent of this variety is so intense as to be overpowering on a still day. Marliac, 1899. (1½-2½ ft (45-75 cm)).

'Sulphurea' (*N. odorata* × *N. mexicana*) This popular, canary-yellow variety has dark-green, heavily mottled foliage. The flowers are star-shaped and only moderately fragrant and the petals are slender and numerous. The stamens are sulphur-yellow in colour. The buds are tall and pointed, and held aloft on stiff, erect peduncles. Marliac, 1879. (1 ft (30 cm)).

'Sulphurea Grandiflora' Award of Merit 1898. This is an improved form, larger in every part and consequently more useful for the average garden pool. This variety is often sold by European nurserymen as *N.* 'Sunrise', but the latter is scarcely mottled and has pubescent petioles and undersides of its leaves. Marliac, 1888. (1½-2 ft (45-60 cm)).

'Turicensis' This bears very fragrant, soft-rose blooms. It is similar to

Figure 3.3 *Nymphaea tetragona* showing Leaf x ½ (a), Flower x ½ (b) and Flower showing 4 Sepals x ½ (c); *N. odorata* showing Leaf x ½ (d), Fruit x ½ (e) and Seed x 3 (f); *N. mexicana* showing Leaf x ½ (g)

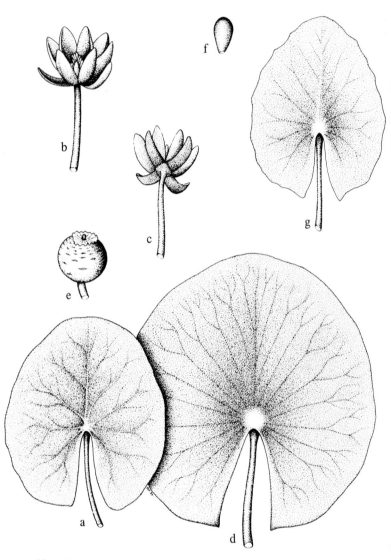

N. odorata var. *rosea*, but with blooms that are smaller and of more intense colouring. (1½-2½ ft (45-75 cm)).

'William B. Shaw' This is one of the choicest *odorata* types. The large, open, creamy-pink flowers have deep-red internal zoning of the narrowly pointed petals. The flowers are very fragrant and held above the water on short, stout stems. The foliage is plain green. Dreer. (1½-2 ft (45-60 cm)).

N. parviflora See *N. alba.*

N. pygmaea See *N. tetragona.*

N. punctata See *N. candida.*

N. reniformis See *N. tuberosa.*

N. semiaperta See *N. candida.*

N. sphaerocarpa See *N. alba* var. *rubra.*

N. sphaerocarpa rosea See *N. alba* var . *rubra.*

N. splendens See *N. alba.*

N. tetragona, N. pygmaea, N. leibergii, N acutiloba, Castalia leibergii, Castalia pygmaea, Pygmy White Waterlily. This is a tiny, white-flowered species with small, dark-green leaves with purple undersides. The blossoms are seldom more than 1 in (2.5 cm) across, are fragrant and with bright golden stamens. The rhizome is erect and entirely devoid of branches. It fruits and sets seed very freely, the young plants raised from seed flowering in their second year. This is a very confused and variable species with many different forms known to botanists. N. America, E. Europe, Asia, Australia. (6 in-1 ft (15-30 cm)).

N. tetragona var. *angustata* The sepals and petals are larger than the type, and the sinus equal or longer than half the length of the leaf. China, Japan.

N. tetragona var. *angustata* f. *indica* The petals are slightly longer than the length of the sepals. It has heavily blotched, brown and green leaves. India.

N. tetragona var. *angustata* f. *orientalis* The outer petals are shorter than the sepals, and the leaves are plain green. China.

N. tetragona var. *grandiflora* This is a larger plant in every part, and was introduced into cultivation by Lagrange in 1900.

N. tetragona var. *himalayense* This very rare form was introduced by Sprenger in 1902, but is now almost certainly lost to cultivation. India.

N. tetragona var. *lata* This is a more diminutive form of the species. Siberia, Kamtschatica, Manchuria.

N. tetragona var. *leibergii* This is the North American form and probably the one most common in cultivation. The leaves are plain green and the white flowers have conspicuous, longitudinal purplish lines down the petals.

N. tetragona 'Helvola' See *N. pygmaea* 'Helvola'.

N. tetragona 'Johann Pring', *N. pygmaea* 'Johann Pring'. The deep-pink flowers are up to 2 in (5 cm) across. The stamens are in two distinct rings, the inner ones pale orange and the outer ones deep pink. The leaves are dark green. This appeared as a pink mutation at Missouri Botanical Gardens and was subsequently developed by George Pring to its present form. 1942. (6 in-1 ft (15-30 cm)).

Nymphaea tuberosa, N. reniformis, N. blanda, N. maculata, Magnolia

Figure 3.4 *Nymphaea tuberosa* showing Seedling x 2 (a) and Seedling with Primary Root (1) and Adventitious Root (2) x 3 (b); *Nuphar advena* showing Germinating Seed x 3 (c), Seedling x 3 (d) and Seedling with Primary Root, beginning Adventitious Root and First True Leaf x 3 (e)

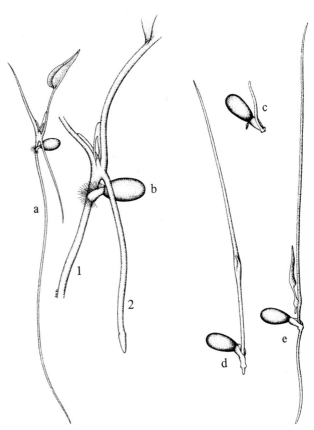

Waterlily. This strong-growing, almost scentless species has pure-white, cup-shaped flowers 4 to 6 in (10 to 15 cm) across. Under normal growing conditions these float on the water, but when crowded are held aloft on stout peduncles. Its petals are almost spathulate and concave, and there are four bright-green sepals. The large, green, orbicular leaves are devoid of the purplish colouring commonly seen in *N. odorata* and its forms. The petioles are green with longitudinal reddish stripes, and in the young foliage are pubescent. The rhizomes are horizontal and fleshy, and if cut in section have the starchy appearance of a potato tuber. It is much branched, the fragile branches being easily detached. N. America. (2-3 ft (60-90 cm)).

N. tuberosa var. *carnea* This pink sport is seemingly lost to cultivation. (2-3 ft (60-90 cm)).

Figure 3.5   *Nymphaea tuberosa* showing Rootstock with Tubers x ¼ (a),
Diagram of Cross-section of Rootstock x ½ (b), Peltate Leaf x ¼ (c), Flower
x ½ (d), Fruit x ½ (e), Seed in Thin Sac x 3 (f) and Seed x 3 (g)

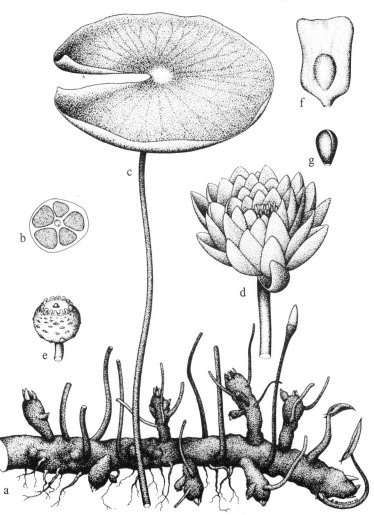

N. tuberosa var. *flavescens*, *N. marliacea* 'Chromatella'.

N. tuberosa var. *maxima* (*Nymphaea odorata* × *N. tuberosa*?) This is
a very vigorous and handsome waterlily. The large, pure-white
blooms appear amidst an abundance of fresh-green foliage.
Suitable only for large pools or lakes. New Jersey. (2-4 ft (60 cm
- 1 m 25 cm)).

N. tuberosa var. *parva* This name was suggested by Charles Abbot in
1888 for a pink form of *N. tuberosa* local to his New Jersey
home, but as far as can be ascertained his suggestion was not
taken up by botanists.

33

N. tuberosa var. *plena* This is a form in which the large white flowers have numerous fluted petals. Some consider this to be akin to *N. tuberosa* 'Richardsonii'. (2-3 ft (60-90 cm)).

N. tuberosa var. *robusta* This is said to be a robust form of *N. tuberosa*, but I have not come across it.

N. tuberosa var. *rosea* (*N. odorata* var. *rosea* X *N. tuberosa*?) Certificate of Merit Massachusetts Horticultural Society 1894. This strong-growing pink form has sweetly scented flowers with bright-red stamens. The leaves are pale-green with longitudinal red stripes on the petioles and peduncles, and the plant is inclined to be rampant. (2-4 ft (60 cm-1 m 25 cm)).

Figure 3.6
Nymphaea tuberosa

N. tuberosa var. *rubra* This is similar in habit to *N. tuberosa* var. *rosea* but a rich rosy-red colour with bright-red stamens. It is extremely fragrant and the foliage abundant and rather excessive. A selection which was introduced by Sturtevant in 1901. (2-4 ft (60 cm-1 m 25 cm)).

N. tuberosa 'Paeslingberg' The large pure-white flowers like waxy goblets float amidst soft-green leaves. It is very vigorous and suitable only for the larger pool. Buggele. (2-6 ft (60-90 cm)).

N. tuberosa 'Richardsonii' This robust cultivar produces large globular flowers with conspicuous pea-green sepals and golden stamens. It is excellent for the large pool. Richardson. 1894. (2½-3½ ft (75 cm-1 m 5 cm)).

Nymphaea urceolata See *N. alba.*

Nymphaea venusta See *N. alba.*

Nymphaea wenzelii See *N. candida* var. *wenzelii.*

CHAPTER 4

Hardy Hybrids

All the hybrids included in this chapter are of unknown, only partially discernible origin, or do not fall within the embrace of a species. Marliac's two distinctive groups of *laydekeri* and *marliacea* hybrids, and the *pygmaea* varieties, are treated as individual sections, whereas the others are merely listed in alphabetical order. Neighbouring varieties, therefore, will not necessarily possess the same or even similar botanical characteristics.

'Aflame' See *Nymphaea* 'Escarboucle'.

'Alaska' This recent introduction has flowers up to 6 in (15 cm) across, extremely wide petals and a dense boss of long, yellow stamens. It is extremely hardy. (2-3 ft (60-90 cm)).

'Albatross' This is medium growing with large, pure-white blooms surrounding a central boss of golden stamens. The leaves are purplish when young but change to deep green when fully expanded. Marliac, 1910. (1-2 ft (30-60 cm)).

'Amabilis' *N.* 'Pink Marvel'. The large, stellate, salmon-pink flowers are up to 10 in (25 cm) across, and deepen to soft rose with age. The yellow stamens also intensify to a fiery orange. The leaves are large and deep green. Marliac, 1921. (1½-2 ft (45-60 cm)).

Figure 4.1
Nymphaea
'Amabilis'

Figure 4.2
Nymphaea
'Andreana'

'Andreana' (*N. alba* var. *rubra* X *N. mexicana*). The deep, brick-red, cup-shaped blooms are up to 8 in (20 cm) across, and streaked and shaded with cream and yellow. They are supported on stout stems 3 or 4 in (7 or 10 cm) above the water. The bold, glossy-green foliage is blotched with maroon and characterised by overlapping lobes. Marliac, 1895. (2-3 ft (60-90 cm)).

'Apple Blossom' See *N. marliacea* 'Carnea'.

'Arc-en-ciel' This extraordinary hybrid has leaves that are splashed with purple, rose, white and bronze. The flowers, which are soft blush-pink, are sweetly scented, but only infrequently produced. The sepals are splashed and stained with rose. It is normally grown for its foliage alone. Marliac, 1901. (1½-2 ft (45-60 cm)).

'Arethusa' (*N. alba* var. *rubra* X *N. mexicana*?). Some authorities suggest this is a hybrid attributable to Marliac, while others describe it as a selection from established cultivars chosen by Dreer. However, no matter where it came from it is a singularly beautiful *Nymphaea* with large, rounded, deep rose-pink flowers intensifying to crimson towards the centre. The rose-pink outer petals are tipped with light red. (1½-2 ft (45-60 cm)).

'Atropurpurea' Award of Merit 1906. The deep-crimson blooms with a satiny violet sheen float amidst handsome dark-green leaves. Each blossom is upwards of 6 in (15 cm) in diameter with pale yellow stamens and incurving petals. The juvenile foliage is dark red, but changes to green with age. Marliac, 1901. (1-1½ ft (30-45 cm)).

'Atrosanguinea' This is a small, bright-red cultivar, and is almost identical in shape and form to the preceding. Marliac. (1-1½ ft (30-45 cm)).

'Attraction' Award of Merit 1912. The large garnet-red flowers of this variety are attractively flecked with white, and may be 9 in (23 cm) or so across when fully expanded. Its rich mahogany stamens are tipped with yellow, and the sepals are of a dirty-white infused with rose-pink. The large foliage is green. Marliac, 1910. (2-4 ft (30 cm-1 m 20 cm)) (Fig. 4.8).

'Aurora' This charming little plant has purplish mottled leaves and flowers that change colour day by day. The buds are cream, opening to yellow, and finally passing through orange to blood-red. It is thought to be the result of a union between *N. alba* var. *rubra* and *N. mexicana*. Marliac, 1895. (1-1½ ft (30-45 cm)).

'Baroness Orczy' This has large, deep rose-pink, cup-shaped blooms, and is excellent for the medium-sized pool. Marliac, 1937. (1½-2 ft (45-60 cm)).

'Bateau' This small-growing variety has fully double, scarlet blossoms. Marliac. (1-1½ ft (30-45 cm)).

'Bory de Saint Vincent' This produces large, vivid-red flowers and deep-green foliage. Marliac, 1937. (2-3 ft (60-90 cm)).

'Brackleyi rosea' The sweetly scented, rose-pink blooms age to flesh pink or almost white, and are held well clear of the water on short, stout stems. The deep-green foliage is very brittle. Seedlings of varying shades of pink and rose are sometimes offered. It was introduced sometime prior to 1909. (2-3 ft (60-90 cm)).

'Brydonia Elegans' See *N.* 'James Brydon'.

'Buggele' See *N. odorata* 'Roswitha'.

'Candidissima' *N. alba candidissima*. This robust, creamy-white variety is believed to be a hybrid between *N. alba* and *N. candida*, or a *N. marliacea* form. The flowers are waxy, with broad petals and no discernible fragrance, and the leaves are rounded with overlapping lobes. (2½-3 ft (75-90 cm)).

'Candidissima rosea' This is a very free-flowering, soft-pink form. (2½-3 ft (75-90 cm)).

'Cardinal' The large blooms are of an intense crimson, borne amidst dark-green leaves. It is very floriferous during sunny weather, but inclined to 'sulk' during a dull summer. (1½-2 ft (45-60 cm)).

'Carisbrookii' (Sometimes listed as *N.* 'Carishbrookii'). The fragrant flowers are a delicate rose-pink, and it has soft green leaves.

(1 ft (30 cm)).

'Charles de Meurville' This extremely strong-growing plant has large, plum-coloured blooms tipped and streaked with white, but ageing to deep wine. The foliage is a handsome olive-green. Marliac, *c*. 1931. (2-4 ft (60 cm-1 m 20 cm)).

'Chromellia' This little-known cultivar has soft yellow petals and orange stamens. The flowers are held well above the surface of the water and produced in abundance, but it is only satisfactory in sunny climates. (1½-2 ft (45-60 cm)).

'Chrysantha' This small-growing waterlily has tiny, reddish-yellow flowers which intensify to scarlet with age. Marliac, 1905. (1 ft (30 cm)).

'Clarissa' The tiny, red flowers are produced in abundance throughout the summer, and it is excellent for a tub or small pool. (1-1½ ft (30-45 cm)).

'Col. A.J. Welch' This is a large and rather coarse waterlily with soft canary-yellow flowers, and generally produces too much foliage to be really satisfactory. It occasionally reproduces viviparously. Marliac. (2-4 ft (60 cm-1 m 20 cm)).

'Collosea' This is possibly the largest and strongest-growing pink variety. The leaves are dark olive-green, and crowned with fragrant flesh-pink blooms. There is also a strain called 'Hammonia'. Marliac, 1901. (2-6 ft (60 cm-1 m 85 cm)).

'Comanche' The small, deep-orange blooms change to bronze with age, and are held well clear of the water. The leaves are purplish when young, rapidly turning to green as they unfurl. Marliac, 1908. (1-1½ ft (30-45 cm)).

'Comte de Bouchard' Masses of small, purplish-red blooms with vivid-orange stamens are produced throughout the summer. Lagrange, 1904. (1-2 ft (30-60 cm)).

'Conqueror' Award of Merit 1912. The large, crimson, cup-shaped flowers are flecked with white. They have broad, incurving petals, bright-yellow stamens and conspicuous sepals with white interiors. The young foliage is purple, eventually changing to green. Marliac, 1910. (1½-2 ft (45-60 cm)).

'Constans' See *N. constans*.

'Crystal White' See *N*. 'Gonnere'.

'Darwin' The fragrant red flowers are heavily striped with longitudinal bands of white, and it has soft green foliage. Marliac, 1909. (1½-2½ ft (45-75 cm)).

'Dawn' This is possibly derived from *N. odorata*. It bears large, extremely fragrant, white blossoms with pinkish sepals. (1½-2 ft (45-60 cm)).

'Delicata' *N. alba delicata*. This is a small-growing, white-flowered variety, the outer petals being flushed with rose. It has curious, circular, pea-green leaves, and is probably a hybrid from *N. candida*, although some believe it to be a selection from *N. alba*. Henkel, 1899. (1 ft (30 cm)).

'Dorothy Lamour' (*N. tetragona* X *N. marliacea* 'Chromatella') The small, rounded, yellow blooms have a greenish flush, and are very fragrant. The leaves are oval, 2 in (5 cm) across, olive-green with flecks of crimson, but the undersides are paler, and also splashed with crimson. The submerged foliage is sagittate, pale yellowish-green splashed with maroon above and dark-green beneath. Plant patent No. 2698, 27 December 1966. Thomas. (1 ft (30 cm)).

'Early Bird' This is a chance find with carmine blossoms some 4 in (10 cm) across. The petals are broad and incurving and the stamens a deep orange. (1½-2 ft (45-60 cm)).

'Eburnea' The sweetly scented, pure-white blossoms are overlaid with a tracery of green and pink lines, and the foliage is bright-green. Marliac. (1½-2 ft (45-60 cm)).

'Ellisiana' Award of Merit 1897. The small, wine-red flowers with orange stamens are produced in abundance, and it is one of the easiest and most reliable waterlily cultivars. Marliac, 1896. (1-2 ft (30-60 cm)).

'Erecta' The thin, papery-white, somewhat pointed blooms are held above the water. It is possibly a hybrid between *N. alba* and *N. odorata*, and is very rare in cultivation. (1-2 ft (30-60 cm)).

'Escarboucle' *N.* 'Aflame'. This is the most famous and popular red variety. The large crimson flower up to 1 ft (30 cm) across has a central boss of golden-yellow stamens, and is richly fragrant. It is a truly magnificent plant. Marliac, 1909. (2-6 ft (60 cm-1 m 85 cm)).

'Esmeralda' This has unusual pink-and-white variegated, stellate flowers, and is a 'conversation piece' rather than a plant of garden merit. Marliac, 1916. (1½-2 ft (45-60 cm)).

'Eucharis' The soft rose-pink blooms are splashed and dappled with white. Marliac, 1912. (6 in-2 ft (15-60 cm)).

'Evangeline' The stellate blooms are of a soft flesh-pink, and the foliage is green. Shaw. (1½-2 ft (45-60 cm)).

'Fabiola' The warm, rosy-red blooms are flushed with white, and sport conspicuous nut-brown stamens. The foliage is a deep green. Marliac, 1913. (1½-2 ft (45-60 cm)).

'Flora de Blanca' This strong-growing, white-flowered variety has sharply pointed petals and yellow stamens. It is vigorous, and suited only to large expanses of water. (2-6 ft (60 cm-1 m 85 cm)).

'Formosa' Award of Merit 1912. The large, fragrant, shocking-pink flowers age to pale mauve. The leaves are pale green. Marliac, 1909. (1½-2 ft (45-60 cm)).

Figure 4.3
Nymphaea
'Froebeli'

Figure 4.4
Nymphaea
'Gladstoniana'

'Froebeli' *N. alba froebeli*. This bears deep blood-red flowers with orange stamens and dull, purplish-green leaves. It is one of the most popular and free-flowering varieties for the garden pool, and is very fragrant. Possibly a hybrid derived from *N. alba* var. *rubra*, it is thought more likely to be the result of a rigorous selection programme organised by the Zurich nurseryman Otto Froebel with seedlings of *N. alba* var. *rubra*. (1½-2 ft (45-60 cm)).

'Fulva' This unusual, small-growing variety has thin coppery-red pointed blooms spotted with pale yellow and canary-yellow sepals with purplish staining. The foliage is green, and spotted with chocolate above and rose beneath. It is an old form which has been superseded by the more modern *N. pygmaea* hybrids. Marliac, 1894. (1 ft (30 cm)).

'Galatee' The white flowers are heavily overlaid with red, producing an extraordinary piebald effect. The dark-green leaves are splashed with maroon. Marliac, 1909. (1½-3 ft (45-90 cm)).

'Gladstoniana' *N.* 'Gladstone', of the trade. Award of Merit 1911. The exceptionally large, pure-white flowers are like huge, floating soup dishes. The broad, curved petals of a thick, waxy texture surround a cluster of golden, thread-like stamens which are slightly fragrant. The large, dark-green, circular leaves have leaf stalks that are distinctly marked with brown. This started as a seedling from *N. tuberosa* selected by George Richardson in 1894. It is believed that this was then crossed with *N. alba*. Richardson, 1897. (2-8 ft (60 cm-2 m 50 cm)).

'Gloire de Temple sur Lot' This really choice variety was dubbed by Marliac 'Queen of the Waterlilies' and named after his home in France. The fragrant, fully double flowers have rosy-pink, incurving petals — a hundred or more to each bloom — and change to pure white with age. The stamens are bright yellow. It is a shy bloomer for the first two or three years, but is well worth establishing. Marliac, 1913. (1½-3 ft (45-90 cm)).

'Gloriosa' *N.* 'Glory'. Award of Merit 1898. The very fragrant flowers of deep currant-red float on the surface of the water. Each blossom is 6 in (15 cm) or more across with five conspicuous sepals and a cluster of bright, reddish-orange stamens. The leaves are orbicular and of a dull, bronzy green. It is a most adaptable and easy-going plant. Marliac, 1896. (1½-3 ft (45-90 cm)).

'Glory' See *N.* 'Gloriosa'.

'Golden Cup' See *N. marliacea* 'Chromatella'.

'Goliath' The large, tulip-shaped flowers have unusual creamy-white stamens. The outer petals are white with a rosy blush, and shade into apricot petaloids towards the centre. Marliac, 1912. (2-6 ft (60-90 cm)).

'Gonnere' *N.* 'Crystal White'. The double, pure-white, globular flowers have conspicuous green sepals. The luxuriant pea-green leaves have a remarkably small spread. One parent was thought to be a seedling of *N. tuberosa* 'Richardsonii'. Marliac. (1½-2½ ft (45-75 cm)).

'Gracillima Alba' This old variety is now probably lost to cultivation. The pure-white flowers are up to 6 in (15 cm) across with curious, narrow spidery petals. The foliage is bright-green splashed and stained with chocolate or maroon. Marliac, 1901. (1½-2 ft (45-60 cm)).

'Graziella' The orange-red flowers are scarcely 2 in (5 cm) across, have deep orange stamens and are produced in abundance throughout the summer. The olive-green leaves are blotched with brown and purple. This is an ideal waterlily for sink or tub culture. Marliac, 1904. (1-2 ft (30-60 cm)).

'Hal Miller' (*N.* 'Virginalis' X *N.* 'Sunrise'). This very vigorous hybrid is similar in character to *N.* 'Sunrise', but a rich creamy white. Miller. (2-6 ft (60 cm-1 m 85 cm)).

'Hammonia' This is a strain of *N.* 'Collosea', which see.

'Hasell' This vigorous yellow variety has pointed, long-petalled flowers up to 6 in (15 cm) across, and is possibly a hybrid between *N. mexicana* and a *N. marliacea* hybrid. (2-3 ft (60-90 cm)).

'Hermine' *N.* 'Hermione'. The tulip-shaped blooms of the purest white are held slightly above the water, and the leaves are dark green and oval. It is believed to be a selection from *N. alba* rather than a hybrid. Marliac, 1910. (1½-2½ ft (45-75 cm)).

'Hermione' See *N.* 'Hermine'.

'Hermosa' The large, fragrant flowers are rose-pink. It is thought by some (notably Lagrange) to be merely a synonym of *N.* 'Brackleyi Rosea'. Henkel, 1904. (1½-2 ft (45-60 cm)).

'Hever White' This has huge, star-shaped flowers and lovely soft green foliage. It is very similar to *N.* 'Gladstoniana', but is less free-flowering in colder districts. Astor, 1937. (2-4 ft (60 cm-1 m 20 cm)).

'Indiana' The orange-red flowers age to deep red, and the foliage is heavily blotched and splashed with purple. Marliac, 1912. (1½-2½ ft (45-75 cm)).

'Irene' This produces rich, rose-red, stellate flowers. (1-2 ft (30-60 cm)).

'J.C.N. Forestier' The bright copper-rose blooms age to deep bronze, and are held well clear of the water. Marliac. (1½-2 ft (45-60 cm)).

'James Brydon' *N.* 'Brydonia Elegans'. Award of Merit 1906. The fragrant, large, crimson paeony-shaped flowers float amidst dark purplish-green leaves that are often flecked with maroon. The stamens are deep orange tipped with bright yellow. It has a characteristic, much-branched rootstock producing few eyes, and is thought to be composed in varying degrees of *N. alba* var. *rubra*, *N. candida* and one of the *N. laydekeri* hybrids. Dreer, 1900. (1½-3 ft (45-90 cm)).

'James Gurney' See *N. marliacea* 'Rubra-Punctata'.

'James Hudson' The dark, wine-red stellate blooms glow with a mauve sheen, and the sepals are white, stained with rose. The foliage is plain green. It was named after a former head gardener of Lord Rothschild. Marliac, 1912. (1½-2½ ft (45-75 cm)).

'Jean de Lamarsalle' The fine-textured blooms are a deep rosy-red, and the large leaves are dark green. It is scarce in cultivation. Marliac. (1½-2½ ft (45-75 cm)).

'Kiss of Fire' The large, rosy-red flowers are produced in abundance, and the foliage is a fresh green. (1½-2½ ft (45-75 cm)).

'Lactea' This has fragrant, flesh-pink flowers changing to creamy-white with age and conspicuous, pea-green sepals. It will flower only in very shallow water, and is possibly derived from *N. odorata*. Marliac, 1907. (1 ft (30 cm)).

Laydekeri hybrids

This is a group of hybrids suitable for the smaller pool which were raised by Marliac and named after his son-in-law Maurice Laydeker. It is believed that one of the parents involved was the small, white-flowering *N. tetragona*. They all produce a profusion of attractive small blossoms and characteristic orbicular leaves. (1-2 ft (30-60 cm)).

laydekeri 'Alba' the snow-white blooms with yellow stamens give off a strong aroma reminiscent of a freshly opened packet of tea.

laydekeri 'Fulgens' The fragrant, bright-crimson flowers have reddish stamens, and the sepals are dark green with rose-blush interiors. The leaves are dark green with purplish undersides, and brown speckling in the region of the petiole. 1895.

laydekeri 'Lilacea' The soft-pink, fragrant flowers age to a deep rosy-crimson. The stamens are a bright yellow and the sepals dark green edged with rose. The glossy green leaves are sparsely blotched with brown.

laydekeri 'Lilacina' See *N. laydekeri* 'Lilacea'.

laydekeri 'Purpurata' This is one of the most outstanding hardy varieties currently available. The rich, vinous-red flowers are produced from late April until the first autumn frosts, and during the height of the flowering season there may be upwards of two dozen blooms on a well-established plant at any one time. The individual blossoms are composed of numerous acutely pointed petals and a striking bunch of bright-orange stamens. The leaves are comparatively small, purple beneath, and often marked on the surface with black or maroon splashes. 1895.

laydekeri 'Red' See *N. laydekeri* 'Fulgens'.

laydekeri 'Rosea' (*N. tetragona* X *N. alba* var. *rubra*?) The deep-rose, cup-shaped flowers age almost to crimson, and are very fragrant, with incurved petals and deep orange-red stamens. The leaves are green above and reddish beneath. The rootstock is upright and not very prolific. An improved and more vigorous form of this cultivar is distributed as *N.* 'Lucida', which see. 1893.

laydekeri 'Rosea Prolifera' A fasciated form of *N. laydekeri* 'Rosea' which was once propagated and distributed, but has long since disappeared.

laydekeri 'Seignourettii' See 'Seignourettii'.

'Leviathan' This vigorous cultivar has large, deep-pink, fragrant flowers and plain green foliage. Marliac, 1910. (2-3 ft (60-90 cm)).

'Livingstone' This small-growing, very fragrant variety bears slender, tulip-shaped blooms of red and white striped petals which surround a central boss of deep-mahogany stamens. Marliac, 1909. (1-2 ft (30-60 cm)).

'Loose' This is a very fragrant American variety with huge, pure-white stellate flowers up to 7 in (18 cm) across held almost a foot (30 cm) above the water. (2-3 ft (60-90 cm)).

'Louise' (*N.* 'Escarboucle' X *N.* 'Mrs C.W. Thomas'). This has deep-red, fully double, cup-shaped blossoms with petals tipped with white. The stamens are yellow and the sepals brownish-green. Plant patent No. 2161, 7 August 1962. Thomas. (2-3 ft (60-90 cm)).

'Lucida' The stellate, rosy-pink blooms intensify to vermilion near the centre. The outer petals and sepals are white flushed with pink, and the stamens are orange. The soft green leaves are splashed with purple. This is an improved form of *N. laydekeri* 'Rosea', which see. Marliac, 1894. (1½-2 ft (45-60 cm)).

'Lusitania' The deep rosy-pink blooms have maroon stamens, and the dark-green leaves are purplish before breaking the surface of the water. Marliac, 1912. (2-3 ft (60-90 cm)).

'Lustrous' This is an extremely fine American hybrid with soft rose-pink petals with a silvery sheen and bright-yellow stamens. The sepals are brown beneath, but with pink interiors, and the young foliage is coppery, turning to dark green with age. It is very free-flowering, and is one of the few cultivars to set seed freely. (1½-2½ ft (45-75 cm)).

'Madame Bory Latour Marliac' This has delicate blooms of soft pink and handsome Lincoln-green foliage. Almost identical to *N.* 'Madame de Bonseigneur', it lacks the pronounced dappling of the blossoms of that variety. Marliac, 1937. (1½-2ft (45-60 cm)).

'Madame de Bonseigneur' The elegant blooms of shell-pink streaked and overlaid with rose-pink give a pleasing dappled effect. Marliac, 1937. (1½-2½ ft (45-75 cm)).

'Madame Julien Chifflot' The large, rich rose-pink, stellate flowers are up to a foot (30 cm) across. The petals are markedly pointed and the stamens bright yellow. It is very free flowering. It has large, plain green leaves. Marliac, 1921. (1½-2½ ft (45-75 cm)).

'Madame Maurice Laydeker' This is a medium-growing variety with globular blossoms of rich cherry-red and large, dull-green leaves. Marliac. (2-3 ft (60-90 cm)).

'Madame P. Cazeneuve' The sweetly scented, deep purplish-rose, cup-shaped blooms are held above the surface of the water. Lagrange. (1½-2 ft (45-60 cm)).

'Madame Wilfron Gonnere' The large, white, cup-shaped blooms are spotted with deep rose, intensifying to soft pink at the centre, and are almost double. This is an outstanding introduction. Marliac. (1½-2½ ft (45-75 cm)).

'Maréchel Pétain' This medium-growing variety has purplish mottled leaves and soft peach flowers, and is similar in stature and colouring to 'Graziella' (1-2ft (30-60 cm))

'Marguerite Laplace' The large, open blooms have rounded rose-pink petals of a thick velvety texture. The foliage is plain green. Marliac, 1913. (1½-2½ ft (45-75 cm)).

'Mark Hanna' This medium-sized, pale-pink variety is now believed to be lost to cultivation. Marliac. (1½-3 ft (45-90 cm)).

'Marliac Flesh' See *N. marliacea* 'Carnea'.

'Marliac Pink' See *N. marliacea* 'Rosea'.

'Marliac Rose' See *N. marliacea* 'Rosea'.

'Marliac White' See *N. marliacea* 'Albida'.

'Marliac Yellow' See *N. marliacea* 'Chromatella'.

N. Marliacea Hybrids

This group of vigorous cultivars are suitable for the medium and large pool. Raised by Marliac, these are of indeterminate origin, but include some of the best and easiest varieties a gardener can grow. It is thought that the parents are likely to include *N. alba, N. alba* var. *rubra* and *N. odorata* var. *rosea*.

N. marliacea 'Albida' *N.* 'Marliac White'. Award of Merit 1887. The large, pure-white, fragrant blooms are held just above the water. The sepals and backs of the petals are often flushed with soft pink, and the large, deep-green leaves have red or purplish

Figure 4.5
Nymphaea alba
(left) and *N.*
marliacea 'Carnea'
(right)

Figure 4.6
Nymphaea
marliacea
'Chromatella'

Figure 4.7
*Nymphaea
marliacea*
'Chromatella'

Figure 4.8
*Nymphaea
marliacea*
'Chromatella'
(foreground); *N.
marliacea* 'Carnea'
(centre right); *N.
alba* (centre left)
and 'Attraction'
(back left)

undersides. 1880. (1½-3 ft (45-90 cm)).

N. marliacea 'Carnea' *N.* 'Marliac Flesh', *N.* 'Mary Exquisita', *N.* 'Morning Glory'. This very strong-growing, flesh-pink hybrid has stellate blossoms 8 or more inches (20 cm) across with golden stamens. The flowers on newly established plants are often white for the first few months. It is an excellent cut-flower variety with a strong vanilla fragrance. The leaves are large, purplish when young and deep green when mature. 1887. (1½-5 ft (45 cm-1 m 50 cm)).

N. marliacea 'Chromatella' *N. marliacea chromatella foliis hepatico-marmoratis*, *N. tuberosa* var. *flavescens*, *N.* 'Marliac Yellow', *N.* 'Golden Cup'. Award of Merit 1895. This is an old and very popular variety with 6-in (15 cm)-wide blossoms of rich canary-yellow. The petals are broad and incurved with deep golden stamens and the pale-yellow sepals are flushed with pink. It is slightly fragrant. The olive-green leaves are boldly splashed with maroon and bronze. Marliac alleged that the parentage included *N. alba* and *N. mexicana*, but botanists at Kew thought it more likely to be a hybrid between *N. tuberosa* and *N. mexicana*, and the name *N. tuberosa* var. *flavescens* was proposed. Another waterlily expert of the time, E.D. Sturtevant, thought *N.* 'Candidissima' was involved. 1887. (1½-2½ ft (45-75 cm)).

N. marliacea 'Flammea' Award of Merit 1897. The fiery-red flowers are flecked with white, the outer petals are deep pink and the stamens a rich orange. The olive-green leaves are heavily mottled with chocolate and maroon. 1894. (1½-2½ ft (45-75 cm)).

N. marliacea 'Ignea' The deep-crimson, tulip-shaped blooms are 6 or more inches (15 cm) across. The anthers are bright crimson, often merging with their background and producing a quite fascinating effect, and the sepals are pale green edged with rose. The foliage is a rich coppery-bronze, changing to dark green with age. There is a slight chocolate-brown mottling of the leaves. 1893. (1½-2½ ft (45-75 cm)).

N. marliacea 'Rosea' *N.* 'Marliac Pink', *N.* 'Marliac Rose'. Award of Merit 1900. Differs only from *N. marliacea* 'Carnea' in the intensity of colouring, its petals being infused with a deep rosy flush. It is very fragrant. The foliage is purplish-green when young, dark green when mature. It is said to have been the first coloured hybrid to be raised by Marliac. 1879. (1½-4 ft (45 cm-1 m 20 cm)).

N. marliacea 'Rubra Punctata' *N.* 'James Gurney'. (Not *N.* 'James Gurney Jnr' – see tropical, night-blooming hybrids, page 83.) The deep rosy-carmine, globular flowers are splashed and spotted with white, the stamens are bright orange, and the sepals a dark olive-green with soft lilac interiors. The foliage is dark green. 1889.

(1½-2½ ft (45-75 cm)).

'Mary Exquisita' See *N. marliacea* 'Carnea'.

'Mary Patricia' This waterlily for the tub or sink garden has beautiful peach-blossom pink, cup-shaped flowers. Johnson. (6 in-1 ft (15-30 cm)).

'Masaniello' The fragrant rose-pink, cup-shaped flowers, liberally sprinkled with flecks of crimson and ageing to deep carmine, are held above the water. The stamens are an intense orange and the sepals white. Marliac, 1908. (1½-3 ft (45-90 cm)).

'Maurice Laydeker' This is one of the smallest varieties. The beautiful vinous-red flowers have faint white flecks on the outer petals. A very shy bloomer and slow propagator, it is worth growing only when *N. pygmaea* 'Rubra' is not available. Marliac. (1 ft (30 cm)).

'Meteor' The crimson flowers are streaked with white which darkens with age; the stamens are bright yellow and the sepals striped with red. The deep-green leaves have purplish undersides. Marliac, 1909. (1½-2½ ft (45-75 cm)).

'Mooreana' See *N.* 'Moorei'.

'Moorei' *N.* 'Mooreana'. (*N. alba* X *N. mexicana*). Award of Merit 1909. This very fine soft-yellow variety was raised at Adelaide Botanic Gardens. The pale-green foliage is irregularly sprinkled with purple spots. It is distinguishable from *N. marliacea* 'Chromatella' by the absence of red stripes on the petioles and flower stems. 1900. (1½-2½ ft (45-75 cm)).

'Morning Glory' See *N. marliacea* 'Carnea'.

'Mrs C.W. Thomas' The extremely fragrant semi-double, shell-pink flowers exhibit characteristics of both *N. odorata* and *N. tuberosa*. The foliage is pale green. It was named by the raisers in honour of their mother, and was the first hardy waterlily for which a patent was applied. 1931. (1½-2½ ft (45-75 cm)).

'Mrs P. Bennett' The intense rose-pink centres shade to shell-pink on the outer petals. (1½-2½ ft (45-75 cm)).

'Mrs Richmond' Award of Merit, 1911. The beautiful pale rose-pink flowers pass to crimson with age. The bases of the petals are bright red, and the stamens a conspicuous golden colour. The sepals are tipped with white. Marliac, 1910. (1½-2½ ft (45-75 cm)).

'Murillo' The immense, crimson, star-shaped blossoms float on the water. The outer petals are tinged with white, and the sepals are white splashed with rose-pink. The foliage is dark green. Marliac, 1910. (1½-2½ ft (45-75 cm)).

'Neptune' The large, stellate, rosy-crimson blooms are spotted with white; the outer petals and sepals are white and the stamens rose.

The purple foliage changes to olive-green with age. Marliac, 1914. (1½-2½ ft (45-75 cm)).

'Newton' The deep rosy-peach flowers with white sepals are held above the water, and the extra-long, pointed petals give the blossoms a star-like appearance. The stamens are a bright orange. Marliac, 1910. (1½-2½ ft (45-75 cm)).

Figure 4.9
Nymphaea 'Mrs Richmond'

'Norma Gedye' The open, semi-double blossoms of deep rose-pink are set amidst rounded, olive-green foliage. It blooms consistently for a greater period of time than most hardy waterlilies. (1-1½ ft (30-45 cm)).

'Noblissima' The dainty flowers of deep irridescent pink are similar in character to *N.* 'Newton'. The foliage is pea-green. Marliac, 1912. (1½-2½ ft (45-75 cm)).

'Odalisque' *N.* 'Opalisque'. This produces masses of medium-sized, rose-pink, stellate blooms ageing to shell pink. The stamens are bright golden and the foliage is light green. I have found this variety to be so prolific as to flower itself to death within two or three years. It must be treated as a temporary inhabitant of the pool and replaced regularly. Marliac, 1908. (1½-2½ ft (45-75 cm)).

'Opalisque' See *N.* 'Odalisque'.

'Orange Blossom' This is a little-known cultivar which I have never seen, although it is sometimes offered in the United States. It is said to have cream flowers with the centre petals of red. The petals are ovate and the stamens deep orange. (1½-2½ ft (45-75 cm)).

'Ozark Queen' This is a selected form with peach-coloured blossoms expanding to orange. It has numerous broad petals and bright orange stamens. (1-2 ft (30-60 cm)).

'Pearl of the Pool' (*N.* 'Pink Opal' X *N. marliacea* 'Rosea'). The clear, fully double, bright-pink blossoms look as if they are made of icing sugar. The stamens are yellow and the orbicular foliage plain green, coppery beneath. Plant patent No. 666, 15 January 1946. Slocum, 1946. (1½-2½ ft (45-75 cm)).

'Phoebus' The yellow flowers are overlaid with crimson and have centres of intense orange-red stamens. The dark-green foliage is heavily mottled with purple. Marliac, 1909. (1-1½ ft (30-45 cm)).

'Phoenix' The bright-red blooms are lined and streaked with pure white, and the foliage is plain green. Marliac, 1913. (1 ft (30 cm)).

'Picciola' This produces large, open, deep-crimson, stellate flowers up to 8 in (20 cm) across held well above the water. The foliage is reddish-green splashed and daubed with maroon. Marliac, 1913. (1½-3½ ft (45 cm-1 m 5 cm)).

'Pink Charm' This has attractive, fully double, pale-pink flowers with yellow stamens and abundant, fresh-green foliage. Slocum, 1947. (1½-2½ ft (45-75 cm)).

'Pink Fashion' The deep-pink flowers have bright-orange stamens. (1-1½ ft (30-45 cm)).

'Pink Giant' This is a distinctive variety with very wide petals and handsome, cup-shaped blooms. (1½-2½ ft (45-75 cm)).

'Pink Glory' The fully double, waxy pink blossoms are up to 6 in (15 cm) across. The stamens are orange. (1½-2½ ft (45-75 cm)).

'Pink Marvel' See *N.* 'Amabilis'.

'Pink Opal' The delicate, cup-shaped blooms of lively coral-pink are held above the water, and the petals are broad and numerous. This is an easily identified variety for the unopened buds are completely spherical and like small marbles. The foliage is green, flushed with bronze. It is a very frail, yet easily grown subject. Fowler, 1915. (1½-2½ ft (45-75 cm)).

'Pink Sensation' This extremely fragrant, free-flowering, pink variety bears starry blooms similar to those of *N.* 'Rose Arey', but which remain open for several hours after those of other hardy cultivars have closed. The individual blooms may be up to 8 in (20 cm) across and have distinctive oval petals some 4 in (10 cm) long. The rounded, deep-green leaves have reddish undersides. Slocum, 1948. (1½-2½ ft (45-75 cm)).

'Pink Star' The stellate, pink blossoms with just a hint of lavender are held above the surface of the water. (1½-2½ ft (45-75 cm)).

'Plenissima' See *N. alba* var. *plenissima*.

'President Viger' This has large, rosy-pink, tulip-shaped blooms and dark green foliage, and is a very choice variety. Marliac, 1906. (1½-2½ ft (45-75 cm)).

'Princess Elizabeth' The blooms are of a delicate cyclamen-pink which intensifies with age, are held well above the water and are very fragrant. This is a seedling from N. 'Brackleyi Rosea'. Perry, 1935. (1½-2½ ft (45-75 cm)).

'Pulva' See N. 'Seignourettii'.

'Punctata' The small, rosy-lilac blooms are flecked with carmine. (1-1½ ft (30-45 cm)).

Pygmaea hybrids The pygmy varieties are excellent subjects for sinks, troughs or pools where the water does not exceed a foot (30 cm) in depth, or on the deeper marginal shelves of a larger pool. The following hybrids are thought to be the result of crosses between N. *mexicana* and N. *tetragona* together with other hybrids to give the various colour breaks. Marliac was a pioneer in the search for good miniature varieties, but the methods which brought him results were never made known.

pygmaea 'Alba' This is the tiniest white waterlily. Each delicately scented bloom measures no more than an inch (2.5 cm) across, and is a complete replica of its larger cousins. The small, oval, dark-green leaves have purple reverses. Closely related to N. *tetragona*, it is collected under the umbrella of that species by some botanists.

pygmaea 'Helvola' N. *tetragona* 'Helvola', N. 'Pygmy Yellow'. The beautiful canary-yellow flowers with orange stamens are produced continuously throughout the summer. The olive-green foliage is heavily mottled with purple and brown. Marliac, 1879.

pygmaea 'Hyperion' The tiny flowers are the deepest amaranth. It is seldom seen in cultivation today. Perry, 1937.

pygmaea 'Johann Pring' See N. *tetragona* 'Johann Pring'.

pygmaea 'Rubis' This is a larger and rarer variety than N. *pygmaea* 'Rubra'. Many authorities consider it to be identical to N. 'Maurice Laydeker', but it is devoid of the white flecks commonly seen on the outer petals of that variety. It is rarely seen outside botanical gardens. Marliac, 1925.

pygmaea 'Rubra' The tiny, blood-red flowers with orange stamens float amidst purplish-green leaves that have distinctive reddish undersides. It is slow to propagate. Some authorities believe it to be the result of a union with N. *alba* var. *rubra*.

'Pygmy Yellow' See N. *pygmaea* 'Helvola'.

'Queen of the Whites' This pure-white cultivar has thick textured, double flowers produced from rounded buds and handsome mid-green foliage. (1½-2½ ft (45-75 cm)).

'Radiance' The fragrant flowers are of glowing shell-pink, deepening towards the centre with sharply pointed incurving petals. Shaw, 1930. (1½-2½ ft (45-75 cm)).

Figure 4.10
*Nymphaea
pygmaea*
'Helvola'

'Rembrandt' This is a strong-growing plant with handsome, rose-pink blooms that age to bright currant red. (1½-2½ ft (45-75 cm)).

'René Gérard' The broad, open flowers with narrow rose-pink petals are blotched and splashed with crimson towards the centre. The foliage is plain green. Marliac, 1914. (1½-2½ ft (45-75 cm)).

'Robinsonii' See *N.* 'Robinsoniana'.

'Robinsoniana' *N.* 'Robinsonii'. (*N. alba rubra* X *N. mexicana*?). Award of Merit 1896. The stellate blossoms have a boss of orange-red stamens, the orange-red outer petals shading to soft yellow at the centre. The sepals are pale green outside and soft pink inside. The olive-green foliage has purple mottling. A distinctive feature of this cultivar is a crimped notch on the lobes on each side of the leaf sinus. It likes shallow water and plenty of sun, and was named in honour of the distinguished gardener Mr W. Robinson. Marliac, 1895. (1½ ft (45 cm)).

'Rosanna Supreme' The large, double, rose-pink, tulip-shaped blossoms display a bold boss of golden stamens, the outer petals being tipped with white. It is very vigorous. Randig. (2-6 ft (60 cm-1 m 85 cm)).

'Rose Arey' Award of Merit 1937. This is the best of the rose-pink varieties. The large, open, stellate flowers have a central boss of golden stamens and an overpowering aniseed fragrance. The fine green leaves are tinged with red, and the juvenile foliage is crimson. It was named after a cousin of Mrs. Fowler. Fowler, 1913. (1½-2½ ft (45-75 cm)).

'Rose Magnolia' The soft pink, more-or-less stellate flowers are held above the water. The small, refined leaves are pale green. It is thought to be a selected seedling of *N. tuberosa* var. *rosea*. (1-1½ ft (30-45 cm)).

'Rose Nymph' (Also called *N.* 'Rosen Nymphe'). This exceptionally fine pink variety produces large, fragrant flowers some 6 in (15 cm) across. The foliage is pale green. It is a choice plant that requires careful cultivation, and is probably derived from *N. odorata*. Junge. (1-1½ ft (30-45 cm)).

'Rosita' This has pale, plum-coloured, stellate flowers, is not very inspiring, and is seldom offered by nurserymen. Marliac, 1908. (1½-2½ ft (45-75 cm)).

'Rosy Morn' The large, stellate, shell-pink flowers are richly fragrant and it is probably a hybrid from *N. odorata*. Johnson, 1932. (1½-2½ ft (45-75 cm)).

'Sanguinea' Award of Merit 1900. This small-growing variety bears medium-sized, blood-red blooms etched with white. The petals are very broad and the stamens a deep orange. The olive-green foliage is spotted with brown. Marliac, 1894. (1 ft (30 cm)).

'Seignourettii' *N. laydekeri* 'Seignourettii', *N.* 'Pulva'. The bright, orange-red flowers with a buff reverse are held high above the water. The foliage is green spotted with chestnut. It is slow to propagate. Marliac, 1893. (1½-2½ ft (45-75 cm)).

'Senegal' This recent introduction has enormous, bright-red blooms up to 8 in (20 cm) across. (1½-2½ ft (45-75 cm)).

'Sioux' Almost identical to *N.* 'Aurora', the pale-yellow blooms pass through orange to crimson, the individual petals being acutely pointed and delicately spotted with red and the stamens yellow. The foliage is purplish mottled. Marliac, 1908. (1-1½ ft (30-45 cm)).

'Sirius' The large, deep rosy-red flowers display glowing crimson stamens, and the sepals are white splashed with red. The handsome, reddish-green foliage is stained with chocolate and purple. Marliac, 1913. (2-3 ft (60-90 cm)).

'Solfatare' This has soft yellow, stellate blooms with a rosy-red flush and dark-green foliage splashed and stained with maroon. Marliac, 1906. (1-2 ft (30-60 cm)).

'Somptuosa' This early-flowering waterlily produces large, fragrant, double, pink blooms. The stamens are vivid orange and contrast markedly with the soft velvety petals. Marliac, 1909. (1½-2 ft (45-60 cm)).

'Souvenir de Fridolfing' The blooms are enormous and pure white. It is suitable only for large expanses of water. Marliac. (2-5 ft (60 cm-1 m 50 cm)).

'Souvenir de Jules Jaquier' The large, globular flowers are of a deep lilac-pink, and the foliage is purplish-green. Marliac, 1921. (1½-3½ ft (45 cm-1 m)).

'Speciosa' This variety produces medium-sized, flesh-pink blooms and green foliage. Marliac. (1½-2 ft (45-60 cm)).

'Splendida' (Also called N. 'Splendide'). The dark-red flowers have orange stamens, and the foliage is a dull green. Marliac, 1909. (1½-2½ ft (45-75 cm)).

'Sultan' The bright, cherry-red flowers have irregular longitudinal streaks of white, and the leaves are dark green. Marliac, 1910. (1½-2½ ft (45-75 cm)).

'Sunburst' The pale-pink blooms with their orange stamens are 6 in (15 cm) or so across and intensify to rose towards the centre. (1-2 ft (30-60 cm)).

'Sunrise' This outstanding yellow variety is of American origin. The large, fragrant, soft canary-yellow blooms are up to 8 in (20 cm) across. The dull-green, elliptical leaves are occasionally blotched with brown, and have reddish undersides and undulating margins. The undersides of both the leaves and petioles are pubescent. (1½-3 ft (45-90 cm)).

'Superba' This is an extremely large-flowering, white variety with golden stamens. The foliage is a fresh pea-green. (2-4 ft (60 cm-1 m 20 cm)).

'Sylphida' The blooms are deep red with the outer petals streaked and flecked with white. (1½-2½ ft (45-75 cm)).

'Tove' This is a very fine white variety with huge blooms sweetly scented reminiscent of those of a cactus dahlia. The outer petals are tinged with rose. Larsen, 1913. (1½-2½ ft (45-75 cm)).

'Tulipiformis' The enormous, tulip-shaped blooms have widely extending soft rose petals. Marliac. (1½-3 ft (45-90 cm)).

'Un Maréchal' This variety bears exquisite blooms of intense camellia-pink and light-green leaves. Marliac. (1½-2½ ft (45-75 cm)).

'Venusta' The large, rose-pink flowers with their orange-yellow stamens are held well above the surface of the water. It is probably derived from N. odorata. Marliac, 1910. (1½-2½ ft (45-75 cm)).

'Vera Louise' This is a gigantic, soft pink hybrid of similar growth to N. 'Gladstoniana'. (2-5 ft (60 cm-1 m 50 cm)).

'Vésuve' *N.* 'Vesuvius'. The large, amaranth flowers are flecked and shaded with orange, and the stamens are red. The juvenile leaves are reddish-green, turning to dark green with age. Marliac, 1906. (1-1½ ft (30-45 cm)).

'Vesuvius' See *N.* 'Vésuve'.

'Virginia' (*N.* 'Sunrise' X *N.* 'Gladstoniana'). The broad, white, starry blossoms are 6 in (15 cm) across, and the sepals are green infused with brown. The orbicular leaves are green above and reddish beneath. Plant patent No. 2172, 18 September 1962. Thomas. (2-4 ft (60 cm-1 m 20 cm)).

'Virginalis' This is a real gem for the medium-sized pool. It bears wonderful semi-double flowers of the purest white. The sepals are rose tinged towards their bases and the stamens bright yellow. The foliage is green flushed with purple. It is slow to become established, but is well worth waiting for. Marliac, 1910. (1½-2½ ft (45-75 cm)).

'Vomerense' This seldom grown miniature variety has tiny, white flowers, and is very similar to *N. pygmaea* 'Alba'. Sprenger, 1904. (6 in-1 ft (15-30 cm)).

'William Doogue' The large, shell-pink, cup-shaped flowers fade to white with age. The sepals are bright pink and the stamens a striking golden colour. The foliage is large and green with occasional brownish splashes. Dreer, 1899. (2-3 ft (60-90 cm)).

'William Falconer' This variety bears medium-sized, upright, blood-red flowers with yellow stamens. The foliage is purplish when young but changes to deep olive-green with age and has distinctive red veins. It was named after the one-time curator of the Botanic Gardens, Cambridge, Massachusetts. Dreer, *c*. 1899. (1½-2½ ft (45-75 cm)).

CHAPTER 5

Tropical, Day-blooming Species

The tropical, day-blooming species of *Nymphaea*, although very attractive in themselves, are not grown as often as the many fine hybrids which they have sired. This is unfortunate, for a number of the smaller kinds in particular are excellent tub plants for greenhouse culture. While it is true that they often lack the brilliant colour and strong constitution of their progeny, their delicate flowers in subtle shades, often with a sweet, rich fragrance, have a grace and charm beyond compare.

Like their hardy counterparts, the tropical diurnal species open their blossoms during late morning and close them as the sun goes down. However, for the most part they are not worthy of consideration for cut-flower decoration, so when this is the intention the large-flowering hybrids should be grown.

The following species are arranged in alphabetical order, although hybrids derived directly from, or attributable to, a species are retained within the confines of that species. Hybrids derived from a union of two species, or one known species and an unknown parent, will be located in Chapter 7, entitled 'Tropical, Day-blooming Hybrids'. As with the hardy species, the figures in parentheses following a description refer to the depth of water in which that species is best grown. This is of academic interest with some kinds as they are difficult to locate in cultivation, but is indicative of the conditions under which they are usually found in the wild.

Nymphaea ampla, Castalia ampla, 'Nymphaea ampla' of the nursery trade is often the nocturnal *N. amazonum*. Dot Leaf. This delightful species bears glistening white, stellate blooms 3 to 6 in (8 to 15 cm) across on stout stems well above the water. The petals are broad, the outer ones infused with lime-green, the sepals coarse and flecked and etched with black, and the stamens yellow. The leaves have wavy margins, are very large, up to 18 in (45 cm) across, green above, purple beneath, with prominent veins and conspicuous, small, black irregular spots. Southern United States, Mexico, Brazil, West Indies. (1½-2½ ft (45-75 cm)).

N. ampla var. *gerardiana* This has much larger blossoms than the type held well above the water, and is thought to be a mutant. (1½-2 ft (45-60 cm)).

N. ampla var. *pulchella* This bears much smaller, white blossoms with fewer stamens. The leaves are scarcely waved and the veining on the undersides is less prominent. West Indies, South America. (1-1½ ft (30-45 cm)).

N. ampla var. *rosea* See *N. flavo-virens* 'Rosea Perfecta'.

N. ampla var. *rudgeana* See *N. rudgeana*.

N. ampla var. *speciosa* The medium-sized, white flowers are slightly smaller than the type. The leaves are more flaccid than the species and with outward pointing teeth along the margins. Mexico, Brazil, West Indies. 1801. (1-1½ ft (30-45 cm)).

N. astraea See *N. flavo-virens* 'Astraea'.

N. baumii See *N. heudelotii.*

N. burttii This produces medium-sized, fragrant, primrose-yellow flowers with narrowly tapering petals floating on the surface of the water. The sepals are pale green and the stamens orange-yellow. The leaves are large, with undulating margins, plain green above but with reddish-brown spots which gradually fade away, and the undersides are pale green. This species was first noticed in East Africa in 1890, but it was not introduced until 1929. An immature seed pod was sent to Mr George Pring at the Missouri Botanical Garden in September 1929 by Mr B. Burtt, who was a botanist for the Tetse Research Bureau in Tanganyika. From the seeds in this pod one plant was raised, and in June 1930 produced its first flower. It was discovered to be a completely new species and named *N. burttii* in honour of its collector. The impact of its introduction upon the development of tropical waterlily cultivars is discussed in Chapter 9. In itself it is not a very important species as it requires a high temperature in order to prosper, and only propagates freely from seed, although hybrids derived from it can be reproduced from tubers and grown in cooler conditions. Central and East Africa. (1½-2 ft (45-60 cm)).

N. calliantha The clear-pink, or occasionally purple or pale blue, stellate blooms are 6 in (15 cm) across with green or rose sepals marked with black spots along their margins. The stamens are a bright golden yellow. The smooth, rounded foliage is cleft almost up to the petiole, green above, purplish-green beneath. Central and South West Africa. (1½-2½ ft (45-75 cm)).

N. capensis, *N. emirensis*, '*N. coerulea*', '*N. stellata*', '*N. scutifolia*'. Cape Blue Waterlily. Cape Waterlily. This popular and very beautiful species has fragrant, bright-blue, stellate blossoms 6 to 8 in (15-20 cm) across with plain-green sepals and yellow stamens. The large, rounded, undulating foliage is green above, but blotched and splashed with purplish-blue beneath. A form, which grows in Madagascar and was once known as *N. emirensis*, is now included as *N. capensis*, but may be worthy of recognition as a distinct variety of the species. It is easily propagated from seed. South East Africa, Madagascar. 1792. (1½-2½ ft (45-75 cm)).

N. capensis var. *azurea* The flowers are soft blue, and the coarsely toothed leaves are spotted with deep violet. South East Africa. 1897. (1½-2½ ft (45-75 cm)).

N. capensis var. *flore-rubra* See *N. stellata* var. *purpurea*.

N. capensis var. *madagascariensis* Tantamon. This small-growing variety of the species is indigenous to Madagascar. The flowers are blue and complete replicas of the type, and the sepals green. The leaves are small, scarcely 3 in (8 cm) across. The rootstock is starchy and is sometimes used by the locals for food. (1-1½ ft (30-45 cm)).

N. capensis var *zanzibariensis*, *N. zanzibariensis*. Royal Purple Waterlily. Royal Blue Waterlily. The large, fragrant, intense-blue flowers with golden stamens and violet anthers are held high above the water. The sepals are plain green on the outside, purple inside. The foliage is variable, from 6 to 18 in (15-45 cm) across, according to growing conditions. The leaves are leathery, more-or-less orbicular, toothed and with wavy margins, green above and occasionally blotched with brown, purple or violet beneath and with prominent veins. This is a very amenable waterlily that is easily raised from seed. Zanzibar. 1875. (1½-2½ ft (45-75 cm)).

The variety *N. capensis* var. *zanzibariensis* hybridises freely, and several forms have been named and are offered by the nursery trade.

N. capensis var. *zanzibariensis* 'Azurea' This is an excellent, pale-blue hybrid. (1½-2½ ft (45-75 cm)).

N. capensis var. *zanzibariensis* 'Jupiter' This bears large, fragrant, deep purplish-blue blossoms, and the sepals are green with purple interiors. (1½-2½ ft (45-75 cm)).

N. capensis var. *zanzibariensis* 'Rosea' The carmine-pink flowers are infused with red, and the sepals are green. The foliage is flushed red beneath. (1½-2½ ft (45-75 cm)).

N. capensis var. *zanzibariensis* 'Rubra' This hybrid is a deep rose-pink. (1½-2½ ft (45-75 cm)).

N. capensis 'Eastoniensis' This selected seedling of *N. capensis* has blossoms of metallic blue and deeply toothed, ovate leaves. Blomberg (Ames), 1896. (1½-2½ ft (45-75 cm)).

N. citrina See *N. stuhlmannii* var. *citrina*.

N. coerulea, '*N. stellata*', '*N. scutifolia*'. Blue Nile Lotus. Egyptian Lotus. It is important to note at the outset that although *N. coerulea* is commonly called the Blue Nile Lotus, it belongs to the Brachyceras group and not the Lotus group. The beautiful sky-blue flowers are up to 9 in (23 cm) across, with black spotted sepals and held well above the water. It is slightly fragrant, with slender yellow stamens and blue anthers. The rounded, green leaves are purplish beneath and with conspicuous deep-purple spots. The substantial rhizomes are used as food by natives in its natural home. This is one of the easiest tropical species to grow, tolerating quite cool conditions, and is readily reproduced from seed. North and Central Africa. 1802. (1½-2½ ft (45-75 cm)).

N. coerulea var. *albida* See *N. micrantha*.

N. coerulea var. *albiflora*, *N. voalefoka*. This is a white variety devoid of the black markings on the sepals. Egypt. 1888. (1½-2½ ft (45-75 cm)).

N. colorata Blue Pygmy. The small, fragrant flowers are up to 4 in (10 cm) across with broad purple or lilac petals and purple stamens. The numerous dark-green, rounded leaves have purplish-green undersides. This is an excellent tub plant easily raised from seed. Africa. 1938. (1½-2½ ft (45-75 cm)).

N. cyanea See *N. stellata* var. *cyanea*.

N. divaricata This extraordinary and very rare species has foliage which is always entirely submerged, as are many of the curious, violet-blue flowers. Zambia. 1930. (1½-2 ft (45-60 cm)).

N. elegans Senorita Waterlily. This small, yet very free-flowering species, bears powder-blue blossoms sporting conspicuous, golden stamens tipped with blue. The outer petals are white with pale-blue shading, and the sepals are spotted and etched with black. The leaves are dark green above and reddish-purple beneath. This is a good plant for tub culture and can be increased from seed. Southern United States, Mexico. 1850. (1-1½ ft (30-45 cm)).

N. emirensis See *N. capensis*.

N. flavo-virens, *N. gracilis*. Frog Waterlily. The white and very fragrant, stellate flowers are held about a foot (30 cm) above the water, are up to 6 in (15 cm) in diameter and with narrow tapering petals. The stamens are bright yellow, and the sepals green marked with dark lines. The leaves are plain green with deeply toothed margins. It is easily increased from seed or tubers. Mexico, Peru, Brazil. 1893. (1½-2½ ft (45-75 cm)).

Hybrids derived from N. flavo-virens

N. flavo-virens hybridises freely with other tropical species and some very fine cultivars have been derived, particularly from its union with *N. capensis* var. *zanzibariensis*. Although doubtless incorrect to do so, these cultivars are often referred to as *N. flavo-virens* cultivars, i.e. *N. flavo-virens* 'Astraea'.

'Antoinette Chaize' The pale-blue, stellate flowers intensify to royal blue at the tips of the petals. Lagrange, 1908. (1½-2½ ft (45-75 cm)).

'Astraea', *N. astraea*. The stellate blossoms are held high above the water. The petals are blue, fading to white at the base, the stamens yellow with purplish-blue anthers, and the sepals pale green. The leaves are green with purplish undersides. (1½-2½ ft (45-75 cm)).

'Astraea Rosea' This is identical to the blue hybrid, but is a rose-pink colour. (1½-2½ ft (45-75 cm)).

'Azurea', *N. gracilis* 'Azurea'. This is a very fine, pale-blue hybrid. (1½-2½ ft (45-75 cm)).

'Blue Star' See *N. flavo-virens* 'Purpurea'.

'Carnea' This produces rich pink, stellate blossoms, and is probably the *N.* 'Orchid Star' of some catalogues. (1½-2½ ft (45-75 cm)).

'Greyae', *N. greyae*. The blue, stellate blossoms shade to white. Grey. (1½-2½ ft (45-75 cm)).

'Mauvii', *N. mauvii*. The fragrant, white, stellate blossoms are carried high above the water. Henshaw, 1892. (1½-2½ ft (45-75 cm)).

'Mrs C.W. Ward', *N.* 'Red Star'. The rich, rosy-pink flowers of this vigorous hybrid, with their dense clusters of golden stamens tipped with pink, are held high above the water. Tricker. (1½-2½ ft (45-75 cm)).

'Orchid Star' I have not encountered this other than in catalogues, and it is probably *N. flavo-virens* 'Carnea'. (1½-2½ ft (45-75 cm)).

'Pink Star' See *N. flavo-virens* 'Stella Gurney'.

'Purple Star' See *N.* 'Edwin A. Lemp'.

'Purpurea' *N.* 'Blue Star', *N. gracilis* 'Purpurea'. This is a rich, purple-flowering variety with a golden centre and bluish stamens. Sturtevant. (1½-2½ ft (45-75 cm)).

'Red Star' See *N. flavo-virens* 'Mrs C.W. Ward'.

'Rosea Perfecta', *N. gracilis* 'Rosea Perfecta', *N. ampla* var. *rosea*. The large, clear-pink blossoms are held above the water. Sturtevant. (1½-2½ ft (45-75 cm)).

'Rubra', *N. gracilis* 'Rubra', *N.* 'True Red Star'. The deep, rose-pink, stellate blossoms are 8 in (20 cm) or more across, and the stamens are red. Sturtevant. (1½-2½ ft (45-75 cm)).

'Stella Gurney', *N.* 'Pink Star'. The large, light-pink, stellate flowers are held high above the water. The leaves are pale green and on very long petioles. This is a seedling from *N. flavo-virens* 'Mrs C.W. Ward'. (1½-2½ ft (45-75 cm)).

'True Red Star' See *N. flavo-virens* 'Rubra'.

'William Becker' This is an improved form of *N. flavo-virens* 'William Stone' with deeper purplish-blue blossoms. (1-1½ ft (30-45 cm)).

'William Stone' The large, dark-blue flowers shading to amaranth at the centre are held high above the water on brownish flower stalks. The golden stamens are distinctly tipped with blue, and the sepals are green with pale-blue interiors. Tricker, 1899. (1½-2½ ft (45-75 cm)).

N. gigantea, Castalia stellaris, Victoria fitzroyana. The immense, sky-blue flowers, which may attain a diameter of 12 or 15 in (30 or 38 cm) are held a foot (30 cm) or more above the surface of the water. The stamens are pale yellow and the sepals green etched with black but pale blue inside. The leaves are green, orbicular or ovate, up to 2 ft (60 cm) across and with wavy margins, and the undersides are purplish-green. This is a very vigorous species requiring a considerable amount of room and a high temperature. It is easily propagated from seed, but the plants will be variable. Australia, New Guinea. 1852. (2-4 ft (60 cm-1 m 20 cm)).

N. gigantea var. *alba* This white form produces blossoms up to 10 in (25 cm) across. 1947. (2-4 ft (60 cm-1 m 20 cm)).

N. gigantea var. *oaspary* The foliage has divergent sinuses. (2-4 ft (60 cm-1 m 20 cm)).

N. gigantea var. *hookeri* This is a variation of the species for which a name is recorded, but the plant's characteristics do not seem to have been noted. (2-4 ft (60 cm-1 m 20 cm)).

N. gigantea var. *media* This is a smaller and more compact form of the type species. (1½-2½ ft (45-75 cm)).

N. gigantea var. *rosea* This is the soft-pink form. (2-4 ft (60 cm-1 m 20 cm)).

N. gigantea var. *violacea* See *N. violacea*.

N. gigantea 'Albert de Lestang' This cultivar is very similar to *N. gigantea* var. *alba*, except that the blooms are flushed with blue on the first day, and the stamens have a distinct, purplish-red ring at their bases. 1946. (2-4 ft (60 cm-1 m 20 cm)).

N. gigantea 'Hudsoniana' This is a selection rather than a hybrid, although it has been claimed that it is the result of a union between *N. gigantea* var. *hookeri* and *N. stellata*, but without any firm evidence. Hudson, 1893. (2-4 ft (60 cm-1 m 20 cm)).

N. gracilis See *N. flavo-virens*.

N. gracilis 'Azurea' See *N. flavo-virens* 'Azurea'.

N. gracilis 'Purpurea' See *N. flavo-virens* 'Purpurea'.

N. gracilis 'Rosea Perfecta' See *N. flavo-virens* 'Rosea Perfecta'.

N. gracilis 'Rubra' See *N. flavo-virens* 'Rubra'.

N. guineensis See *N. heudelotii*.

N. heudelotii, N. baumii, N. maculata, N. 'Tanganyika' of the trade. The tiny, bluish-white, stellate blossoms an inch (25 mm) or so across are held above the water. The sepals are conspicuously spotted with black. The short, rounded rootstock is about the size of a walnut. This easily grown plant is tolerant of cooler conditions than most, but it is recommended that the plants be allowed a two-month resting period each year. It is easily raised from seed. There is a form, possibly merely geographical, that has been described (1902) as *N. guineensis*, but this does not deserve specific rank nor, according to the botanists, even varietal status. The type species was described in 1853 and introduced in 1900. (1 ft (30 cm)).

N. heudelotii var. *nana* This is possibly the smallest tropical water-lily, with leaves scarcely 2 in (5 cm) across and very small, white blooms. (6 in-1 ft (15-30 cm)).

N. lutea See *N. mexicana*.

N. maculata See *N. heudelotii*.

N. mauvii See *N. flavo-virens* 'Mauvii'.

N. mexicana, *N. flava*, *N. lutea*, *Castalia flava*. The canary-yellow flowers have a slight fragrance, the stamens are yellow. The leaves are rounded, sometimes irregular, green spotted with brown, and infused with red beneath. It is almost hardy and reproduces by suckers or runners. Southern United States. Introduced into Australia. Described in 1832. Introduced into Great Britain in 1881. (6 in-1 ft (15-30 cm)).

N. micrantha, *N. coerulea* var. *albida*, *N. rufescens*. Bulb Leaf. The medium, bluish-white flowers have yellowish sepals spotted with violet, and the stamens are cream. The small, rounded or oval leaves are plain-green above, reddish beneath and spotted with black. A seldom grown species, it has been of immense value in the development of garden hybrids like *N.* 'Panama Pacific' and *N.* 'August Koch'. Strongly viviparous, the young plantlets vary considerably, and at one time were given different names according to the form they took. West Africa. 1846. (1½-2½ ft (45-75 cm)).

N. nelumbo See *Nelumbo nucifera*.

N. nouchali See *N. stellata*? *N. pubescens*?

N. nubica The crimson blossoms have green sepals spotted with maroon, and the leaves are a plain green. It is possibly merely a variation of *N. coerulea*. Africa. 1853. (1½-2½ ft (45-75 cm)).

N. ovalifolia Tabora Waterlily. The fragrant, small, white, stellate blossoms, the petals of which are tipped with blue, are held well above the water. The stamens are bright golden. The leaves are green flecked with maroon and brown above, bluish-green beneath. These are 8 to 10 in (20-25 cm) across, more or less ovate, and produced in abundance. It is a vigorous grower which is easily raised from seed, and is invaluable material for the hybridiser. East Africa. Described in 1882. Introduced into Great Britain in 1914. Forms improved by cultivation often have the name *grandiflora* or *gigantea* appended. (1½-2½ ft (45-75 cm)).

N. pentapetala See *Nelumbo pentapetala*.

N. polychroma Little is known about this species except that it is similar to *N. colorata* and may even be a form of that species. Africa. (1-2½ ft (30-75 cm)).

N. primulina See *N. sulfurea*.

N. rufescens See *N. micrantha*.

N. scutifolia Probably not deserving of specific rank, but it is afforded it by horticulturists. It is believed to be a variety of *N. capensis* with a rhizomatous as opposed to a tuberous rootstock, but said by others to be a variant of *N. coerulea*. Whatever the botanical complexities, the plant sold under this name in the trade has attractive, bright-blue, stellate blossoms. Cape Of Good Hope? (1½-2½ ft (45-75 cm)).

N. stellata, N. nouchali? The beautiful, slightly fragrant, stellate blossoms of blue, or sometimes white, are held high above the water. The type species has mid-blue flowers with pointed petals lightening to pale blue at the base, the stamens are golden, and the sepals minutely spotted with black. The large, orbicular or elliptical leaves have violet undersides and prominent green veins. It reproduces from tubers. South and East Asia, Borneo, Phillipines. (1½-2½ ft (45-75 cm)).

N. stellata var. *bulbifera* See *N.* 'Daubeniana'.

N. stellata var. *cyanea, N. cyanea*. This has slightly fragrant, pale-blue, medium-sized blossoms and wavy foliage. (1½-2½ ft (45-75 cm)).

N. stellata var. *prolifera* See *N.* 'Daubeniana'.

N. stellata var. *purpurea* This is a darker form of the type species. (1½-2½ ft (45-75 cm)).

N. stellata var. *rosea* This soft rose-pink form has long been cultivated. 1869. (1½-2½ ft (45-75 cm)).

N. stellata var. *versicolor* This attractive variety bears blossoms that vary from deep rose-pink to white. The leaves are orbicular or elliptical and undulating being green with pinkish undersides. Each autumn small tubers develop at the point where the leaves join the stem, and it is these that are imported and sold in the aquarium trade as *N. stellata*. Ceylon, India, Philippines. (1½-2½ ft (45-75 cm)).

N. stellata 'Berlin' This is an improved variety with gorgeous, large, sky-blue flowers. (1½-2½ ft (45-75 cm)).

N. stuhlmannii The fragrant, bright-yellow flowers up to 6 in (15 cm) across, have orange stamens and golden anthers, while the sepals are pale green. The leaves are more-or-less circular, up to 10 in (25 cm) across, and with prominent veins. It is seldom encountered in cultivation. Africa. 1890. (1½-2½ ft (45-75 cm)).

N. stuhlmannii var. *citrina, N. citrina*. This is a pale-yellow form. (1½-2½ ft (45-75 cm)).

Nymphaea 'William Falconer'

Nymphaea laydekeri 'Purpurata'

Nymphaea odorata 'Sulphurea'

Nymphaea 'Gloriosa'

Nymphaea 'Albatross'

Nymphaea 'Rose Arey'

Nymphaea stellata

Nymphaea 'Rene Gerard'

Nymphaea 'Froebeli'

Nymphaea 'Indiana'

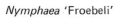

N. sulfurea, *N. primulina*. This small-growing, sweetly scented, yellow-flowered species has purplish stamens. The leaves are ovate, reddish-brown above and red beneath. A useful species for tub culture, it can easily be grown from seed and has played an important part in the production of modern hybrids like *N.* 'Aviator Pring'. Africa. 1900. (1 ft (30 cm)).

N. sulfurea var. *grandiflora* This name is given to a larger selected form of the type. (1 ft (30 cm)).

N. violacea, *N. gigantea* var. *violacea*. This is a violet-coloured water-lily closely allied to *N. gigantea*. There is some discussion as to whether this deserves specific rank. However, in most instances it is referred to by the name given. Australia. (1½-3½ ft (45 cm - 1 m)).

N. vivipara This is the name given to a strongly viviparous plant with medium-sized, white flowers with a bluish or silvery sheen. I have not seen this species either live or as an herbarium specimen and, am inclined to believe it is a synonym of *N. micrantha*, despite the fact that the name not infrequently occurs in the literature. West Africa.

N. voalefoka See *N. coerulea* var. *albiflora*.

N. zanzibariensis See *N. capensis* var. *zanzibariensis*.

CHAPTER 6

Tropical, Night-blooming Species

The night-blooming waterlilies are a fascinating group, opening their blossoms as the sun begins to set and not closing them again until sunrise. On dull overcast days they may remain open during daylight too. As they generally produce flowers on strong stems, they are excellent for cutting for floral decoration. In Great Britain most gardeners treat the night-flowering species and cultivars as perennial, whereas in the United States, where they are more extensively grown, they are usually regarded as annuals.

The following species are arranged in alphabetical order, although hybrids derived directly from, or attributable to, a species are retained within the confines of that species. Hybrids derived from a union of two species, or one known species and an unknown parent, will be located in Chapter 8, dedicated to the tropical, night-blooming hybrids. As with both the hardy and tropical, day-blooming species, the figures in parentheses following a description refer to the depths of water in which that species is best grown. This is of academic interest with some kinds as they are difficult to locate in cultivation, but is indicative of the conditions under which they are usually found in the wild.

Nymphaea albo-viridis See *N. amazonum*.

N. amazonum, N. albo-viridis, '*N. blanda*', *N. ampla* of the nursery trade. The large, sweetly scented, creamy-white flowers about 3 in (8 cm) across have thick velvety petals and cream stamens. The sepals are dark green with pale green interiors. The handsome, oval leaves, are green spotted brown above, reddish-brown spotted black beneath. It is easily reproduced from seed. South America, West Indies. 1832. (1½-2 ft (45-60 cm)).

N. amazonum var. *goudotiana* This variety is identical to the type species, except for a conspicuous ring of long hairs around the flower stems just beneath the blossoms. South America, West Indies. (1½-2 ft (45-75 cm)).

N. amazonum var. *submersum* This form with its entirely submerged foliage was described by Sagot in 1881, but as far as can be ascertained was never introduced into cultivation. South America. (1½-2 ft (45-60 cm)).

'*N. blanda*' See *N. amazonum*.

N. blanda This small-growing species bears brilliant-white, papery blossoms. The stamens are yellow and the sepals green marked with conspicuous crimson lines. The peduncles are covered in hairs. The small, green leaves show prominent veins beneath. It is scarce in cultivation. South America, West Indies, Australia. (1-1½ ft (30-45 cm)).

N. blanda var. *amazonum* See *N. rudgeana*.

N. blanda var. *fenzliana* This larger form has green sepals with yellowish interiors, and the outer petals are yellowish. Guatamala. 1841. (1½-2½ ft (45-75 cm)).

N. coteka See *N. pubescens*.

N. dentata See *N. lotus*.

N. edulis See *N. pubescens*.

N. esculenta See *N. pubescens*.

N. fragrans See *N. gardneriana*.

N. gardneriana, *N. fragrans*, *N. passiflora*. The small, coppery-red blossoms are some 3 or 4 in (8 or 10 cm) across with distinctive mahogany stamens, and the sepals are brownish-green. The leaves are small, ovate and often with crisped margins, the upper surfaces being green, and the undersides spotted with deep maroon. Brazil, Paraguay. (1½-2 ft (45-60 cm)).

N. gibertii *Castalia gibertii*, *Leuconymphaea gibertii*. This small-growing species has tiny, white, scentless blossoms, the outer petals being marked with a tracery of faint, purple lines. It has small, ovate leaves. Paraguay. 1858. (1-1½ ft (30-45 cm)).

N. jamesoniana, *N. sagittariaefolia*. The small, ochre flowers have green sepals marked with crimson lines. The oval or heart-shaped, green foliage has purple markings beneath. Ecuador, Puerto Rica. (1-1½ ft (30-45 cm)).

N. lasiophylla This uninspiring species produces numerous off-white, stellate blooms some 3 in (8 cm) across, with the sepals spotted with black. The large, green leaves have reddish undersides etched with purple lines. Brazil. 1832. (1-1½ ft (30-45 cm)).

N. lotus, *N. thermalis*, *N. ortgiesiana*, *N. dentata*, *Castalia mystica*. White Nile Lotus. The deliciously scented, pure-white flowers are tinged with pink and up to 8 in (20 cm) across. The stamens are bright yellow, the sepals green, and the outer petals lie horizontally. The flower stems are hairy. The large, handsome, green, peltate foliage has toothed edges and prominent veins beneath. It is easily raised from seed or tubers. Egypt, Central and West Africa, Madagascar, Hungary. The Hungarian form is sometimes referred to as *N. thermalis*, but it is a geographical variation and scarcely different from the African type species. An inhabitant of the hot thermal springs of Grosswardein and Kaiserbade, it has been speculated that it may have been introduced. However, it is more likely that it was once more widely distributed and the main populations were driven south by colder conditions, leaving only those growing in the warm water of the springs. This theory is further reinforced by the fact that snails of the same type occur in both Hungary and Africa in the same waters as *N. lotus*. 1802. (1½-2½ ft (45-75 cm)).

N. lotus 'Delicata' See *N.* 'Delicatissima'.

N. lotus var. *dentata* The pure-white flowers have narrow petals and reddish stamens. The foliage is plain green and dentate. Sierra Leone. (1½-2½ ft (45-75 cm)).

N. lotus var. *gigantea* This larger variant of the species was used by Pring in his breeding programme. (1½-2½ ft (45-75 cm)).

N. lotus var. *dentata* 'Grandiflora' This is an improved and larger-flowering variety. Sturtevant. (1½-2½ ft (45-75 cm)).

N. lotus var. *dentata* 'Juno' See *N. lotus* var. *dentata* 'Superba'.

N. lotus var. *dentata* 'Magnifica' This produces large, white flowers with a sprinkling of purplish spots at the base of the golden stamens. Bisset. (1½-2½ ft (45-75 cm)).

N. lotus var. *dentata* 'Superba', *N. lotus* var. *dentata* 'Juno'. This bears pure-white flowers with bright yellow stamens, and is one of the few hybrid waterlilies to come true from seed. (1½-2½ ft (45-75 cm)).

N. lotus var. *monstrosa* This curious form has flower buds which are transformed into tubers and eventually form new plants. It is unlikely to be encountered in cultivation. Lake Nyassa. 1886. (1½-2½ ft (45-75 cm)).

N. lotus var. *pubescens* See *N. pubescens*.
The hybrids *N.* 'Ortgiesiana Alba' and *N.* 'Ortgiesiana Rubra' are also derived in part from *N. lotus*. See Chapter 8.

N. nouchali See *N. pubescens*? *N. stellata*?

N. ortgiesiana See *N. lotus*.

N. oxypetala This rare species is unlikely to be in cultivation. The pale-bluish flowers display a dense central cluster of stamens, and the sepals and petals are strikingly lance-shaped. The thin, crispy foliage is entirely submerged. Ecuador. 1845. (1-1½ ft (30-45 cm)).

N. passiflora See *N. gardneriana*.

N. pubescens, *N. coteka*, *N. esculenta*, *N. edulis*, *N. nouchali*? *N. lotus* var. *pubescens*, *Castalia sacra*, *Castalia edulis*. The small, white flowers have yellow stamens and greenish sepals lined and veined with white. The leaves are dark green with curved margins and purplish undersides. The whole plant is distinctly hairy. The rhizomes grow above soil level, but are firmly rooted. During the dry season, all but the tip of the rhizome withers away, but this resurges into growth as soon as the rains return. India, Java, Philippines, Australia (introduced?). 1803. (1½-2½ ft (45-75 cm)).

N. pulchella See *N. tenuinervia*.

N. rosea See *N. rubra*.

N. rubra, *N. rubra* var. *rosea*, *N. rosea*, *Castalia magnifica*. Red Indian Waterlily. The beautiful, slightly fragrant, deep-red flowers are some 8 in (20 cm) across, with purplish sepals and red stamens. The large leaves, up to 18 in (45 cm) in diameter, are deep purple ageing to plain green, and have toothed margins and pubescent undersides. The type is seldom seen in cultivation. Bengal. 1803. (1½-2½ ft (45-75 cm)).

N. rubra var. *rosea* See *N. rubra*.

N. rubra 'Rosea' This is a free-flowering, slightly paler variety of garden origin, and is the *N. rubra* likely to be encountered in cultivation. It is easily raised from seed. (1½-2½ ft (45-75 cm)).

N. rudgeana, *N. ampla* var. *rudgeana*, *N. blanda* var. *amazonum*, *N. sinuata*, *N. tropaeolifolia*. The greenish-cream blooms have an overpowering lemon fragrance. The sepals are creamy-yellow infused with red, but with greenish interiors; the stamens are also a creamy-yellow. The undulating foliage has toothed margins, and is reddish-green spotted with black. The variety is scarce in cultivation. South America, West Indies. 1853. (1-1½ ft (30-45 cm)).

N. sagittariaefolia See *N. jamesoniana*.

N. sinuata See *N. rudgeana*.

N. stenaspidota The deep-crimson flowers are 3 to 4 in (8 to 10 cm) across with sepals marked with conspicuous lines. The leaves are dark green and almost triangular in outline. A small-growing species, it is unlikely to be encountered in cultivation. Brazil. 1841. (1-1½ ft (30-45 cm)).

N. tenuinervia (Sometimes described as *N. tenerinervia*), *N. pulchella*. This small, stellate-flowered species is known mainly from herbarium specimens. The foliage is oval, with the undersides clearly spotted with black. Brazil. 1894. (1-1½ ft (30-45 cm)).

N. thermalis See *N. lotus*.

N. tropaeolifolia See *N. rudgeana*.

N. zenkeri The tiny, white flowers are about 2 in (5 cm) in diameter, and the sepals are light green with white interiors. The slender, membranous foliage is about 6 in (15 cm) long and 3 in (8 cm) wide with pubescent undersides. West Africa. (1-1½ ft (30-45 cm)).

CHAPTER 7

Tropical, Day-blooming Hybrids

'A.O. Siebert' This is a very free-flowering, rose-pink hybrid. Henkel. 1907. (1½-2½ ft (45-75 cm)).

'Adriana Nannelli' The stellate flowers are a soft blue. (1½-2½ ft (45-75 cm)).

'African Gold' The medium-sized blossoms are an intense yellow and the leaves a fresh green, paler beneath. Pring, 1941. (1-1½ ft (30-45 cm)).

'Afterglow' This has large, fragrant, peach-coloured stellate flowers with soft pink reverses. The leaves are smallish, fresh green with paler undersides. Randig, 1946. (1-2½ ft (30-75 cm)).

'Albert Greenberg' This hybrid bears copper-gold, stellate blossoms and a handsome, mottled foliage. Birdsey. (1½-2½ ft (45-75 cm)).

'Alice Tricker' The broad-petalled flowers are a pure white. It is an improved Nymphaea 'Mrs George H. Pring'. Tricker, 1937. (1½-2½ ft (45-75 cm)).

'American Beauty' (N. flavo-virens 'William Stone' X N. colorata). The immense, pale plum-coloured blossoms have fluorescent yellow centres. The large, orbicular, green leaves have wavy margins and are reddish beneath with prominent green veins. Pring, 1941. (2-3 ft (60-90 cm)).

'Amethyst' The medium-sized blooms are the colour of a glowing amethyst, and it is strongly viviparous. Henkel. (1½-2½ ft (45-75 cm)).

'August Koch' (N. 'Mrs Woodrow Wilson' X N. 'Blue Beauty'?). The fragrant, mid-blue flowers are some 9 in (23 cm) across, and are held well above the water. The sepals are purplish-lilac and the stamens orange. The leaves are dark green above, infused with pink beneath and up to a foot (30 cm) in diameter. It is viviparous, one of the best for cut flowers and a good, winter-blooming variety. Koch (Pring), 1922. (1½-2½ ft (45-75 cm)).

'Aviator Pring' (N. sulfurea X N. 'St. Louis'). The rich-yellow blossoms are held well above the water, and the green, toothed leaves have wavy margins. It was named by Mr George Pring after his son who was killed in the Second World War. Pring. (1½-2½ ft

(45-75 cm)).

'Bagdad' The broad, flat, purplish-blue flowers are produced amidst leaves which are spotted reddish-brown above and striped purple beneath. It is strongly viviparous. Pring, 1941. (2-3 ft (60-90 cm)).

'Beldtmoore' This recent introduction has fully double squarish blossoms of rich purple 6 to 8 in (15-20 cm) across. The golden stamens have purple anthers. (1½-2½ ft (45-75 cm)).

'Berolina' (*N. flavo-virens* X *N. capensis*?). This very free-flowering, deep-blue variety bears individual blossoms 8 in (20 cm) across. (1½-2½ ft (45-75 cm)).

'Black Prince' This produces deep purplish-blue, stellate blooms (1½-2½ ft (45-75 cm)).

'Blue Beauty' *N.* 'Pennsylvania', *N.* 'Pulcherrima'. (*N. coerulea* X *N. capensis* var. *zanzibariensis*). This cultivar has been officially given the name 'Blue Beauty', although crosses were made almost simultaneously by Tricker and Conard and given the names 'Pennsylvania' and 'Pulcherrima' respectively. The results of both unions were the same. Fragrant, deep-blue flowers with a central gold disc from which the yellow stamens and violet anthers arise. The sepals are lined and spotted with black. The leaves are immense, up to 2 ft (60 cm) across, dark-green with brown freckling above, purplish-green beneath, and with wavy margins and long, tapering lobes. 1897. (1½-3 ft (45-90 cm)).

'Blue Bird' This has deep-blue, stellate flowers, and is strongly viviparous. Tricker. (1½-2½ ft (45-75 cm)).

'Blue Independence' This is a blue form of *N.* 'Independence'. Tricker. (1½-2½ ft (45-75 cm)).

'Blue Smoke' The grey-blue blossoms have a silvery sheen, and the leaves are green with purplish mottling beneath. It is a seedling of *N.* 'Green Smoke'. Wood. (1½-2½ ft (45-75 cm)).

'Blue Triumph' The huge, deep-blue flowers are up to a foot (30 cm) across, and are borne above green foliage flecked and spotted with brown. Johnson. (2½-3½ ft (45cm - 1m)).

'Bob Trickett' The large, campanula-blue, cup-shaped blossoms have yellow stamens. The large, orbicular leaves are green above and reddish beneath with prominent green veins. Pring, 1949. (1½-2½ ft (45-75 cm)).

'Cardinalis' The bright red blossoms have broad petals and orange stamens. (1½-2½ ft (45-75 cm)).

'Castaliiflora' (*N. capensis* var. *zanzibariensis forma rosea* X *N. capensis* var. *zanzibariensis forma rosea*). By crossing two pink forms of *N. capensis* var. *zanzibariensis*, and then continuously selecting the best forms, Mr George Pring eventually fixed a good, fragrant, light-pink variety with broad, open blossoms up to 10 in (25 cm) across. The stamens are yellow with pink anthers, and the serrated, green foliage is delicately mottled with reddish-brown above, infused with pink beneath. It can be raised true to type from seed. Pring, 1913. (1½-2½ ft (45-75 cm)).

'Celeste' This produces violet blooms with golden stamens; the unopened buds are lined with pale purple. The large, dark-green leaves are flecked with reddish-brown above, paler and spotted with purple beneath. It is occasionally viviparous. Pring, 1941. (1½-2½ ft (45-75 cm)).

'Chicago' The beautiful clear-pink, stellate blooms shade to sulphur-yellow at the centre, and are held high above the water. The leaves are olive-green splashed with brown. Koch. (1½-2½ ft (45-75 cm)).

'Christine Lingg' The powder-blue blossoms have golden stamens. Lingg. (1½-2½ ft (45-75 cm)).

'City of Gold' See N. 'Eldorado'.

'Cleveland' The blossoms are fragrant, rose-pink and stellate; the leaves are green, splashed and stained with brown. Tricker. (1½-2½ ft (45-75 cm)).

'Clint Bryant' This tall-stemmed, blue-flowered hybrid is a recent introduction named in honour of a well-known American plant photographer. Wood. (1½-2½ ft (45-75 cm)).

'Colonel Lindberg', N. 'Lindy'. The very fragrant, deep-blue flowers are held well clear of the water. The ovate leaves have brown mottling on the upper surfaces, blotched with purple beneath. Tricker, 1929. (1½-2½ ft (45-75 cm)).

'Daisy' The large, open, pure-white flowers display golden stamens which turn pinkish in low temperatures. The leaves are dark green splashed with brown above, pale green beneath. It is strongly viviparous. Pring, 1934. (1½-2½ ft (45-75 cm)).

'Daubeniana' (The alternative spellings for this hybrid are 'Dauben' and 'Daubenyana') N. stellata var. prolifera, N. stellata var. bulbifera. Daubeny's Waterlily. Madagascar Aquarium Lily, Madagascar Dwarf Lily. (N. micrantha X N. coerulea?). The small, blue blossoms are seldom more than 2 in (5 cm) in diameter with a sweet, spicy aroma. The petals are narrow with a greenish cast, the sepals whitish and the stamens yellow. The leaves are ovate or roughly sagittate, brownish-green splashed with choco-late. It is an excellent subject for tub or aquarium, and is strongly viviparous. Daubeny, 1863. (6 in (15 cm)).

'Director George T. Moore' Derived from N. colorata, this hybrid has huge, deep-purple blooms with rich golden centres. The smallish, dark-green leaves are splashed with maroon or brown, and the pale-green undersides are infused with purple. Pring, 1941. (1½-2½ ft (45-75 cm)).

'Edward C. Eliot' This seedling from 'Mrs Edwards Whitaker'

Marmorate Form, has pale-pink, cup-shaped blooms frequently 8 in (20 cm) across. The stamens are yellow with pink anthers, and the unopened buds are green and spotted with dark purple. The leaves are green splashed with reddish-brown above, pale pink beneath. Pring, 1923. (2-3 ft (60-90 cm)).

'Edwin A. Lemp', *N.* 'Purple Star'. The purple, stellate blooms have yellow stamens tipped with pink. (1½-2½ ft (45-75 cm)).

'Eldorado', *N.* 'City of Gold'. The large, lemon-yellow blossoms are fragrant, the leaves ovate and green, with darker mottling. It is one of the hardier tropicals. Randig. (1½-2½ ft (45-75 cm)).

'Elena Grossi' The stellate flowers are of an intense rosy-red. (1½-2½ ft (45-75 cm)).

'Enchantment' The deep salmon-pink blooms are produced in abundance above oval, slightly speckled, pea-green foliage. Randig. (1½-2½ ft (45-75 cm)).

'Evelyn Randig' The fragrant, deep-magenta flowers on stout stems are held above handsome, dark-green leaves which are splashed and striped with chestnut. Randig, 1931. (2-3 ft (60-90 cm)).

'Francis Griffith' This has small, deep-purple blooms with a rich velvety overlay, and is viviparous. Koch. (1-2 ft (30-60 cm)).

'François Treyve' This free-flowering, indigo-blue hybrid is believed to be lost to cultivation. Lagrange, 1910. (1½-2½ ft (45-75 cm)).

'General Macarthur' This prolific variety has yellow blossoms with a pink infusion and green leaves with brown mottling. (1½-2½ ft (45-75 cm)).

'General Pershing' (*N.* 'Mrs Edwards Whitaker' X *N.* 'Castaliiflora'). Silver Medal of the Society of American Florists, 1923. The large, deep-pink, sweetly scented blossoms are held high above the water; the yellow stamens are tipped with pink, and the sepals green, with light-pink interiors. The young buds are green with conspicuous purple stripes, and the large, purplish-green leaves are splashed beneath with red. Pring, 1920. (1½-2½ ft (45-75 cm)).

'Golden Fascinator' This unusual, deep-orange hybrid, with its distinctive coppery edging to the petals is fragrant, and has large, dark-green leaves. Randig, 1946. (1½-2½ ft (45-75 cm)).

'Golden West' The large, fragrant, stellate blooms with their golden stamens change with age from pale pink through gold to apricot, and are held a foot (30 cm) or so above the water. The leaves are green with purplish speckling. It is a seedling from *N.* 'St. Louis'. Randig, 1936. (1½-2½ ft (45-75 cm)).

'Governor Louis Emerson' The huge, light-blue flowers up to a foot (30 cm) across are held high above the water. The sepals are light blue and the leaves olive-green splashed with brown. Koch. (1½-2½ ft (45-75 cm)).

'Green Smoke' This extraordinary, recent introduction, has chartreuse petals shading to light blue at the tips. The leaves are slightly scalloped, bronzy-green with a bronze speckling. Randig. (1½-2½ ft (45-75 cm)).

'Grossherzog Ernst Ludwig' The large, purplish-blue, stellate blooms with yellow centres are held high above the water. It is a rampant grower, which coupled with its almost unpronounceable name no doubt accounts for its lack of popularity. Henkel, 1907. (2½-3½ ft (75 cm-1 m)).

'Gzetta Jewel' This is a strong-growing, soft-pink variety. (2½-3½ ft (75 cm-1 m)).

'Hawaii' The cup-shaped, pink blossoms, with their red stamens, shade to orange. (1½-2½ ft (45-75 cm)).

'Henkeliana' The broad, open, deep-blue flowers smell of fresh violets. Henkel. (1½-2½ ft (45-75 cm)).

'Henry Shaw' (*N.* 'Castaliiflora' X *N.* 'Castaliiflora'). This is really a fragrant, soft blue-flowered *N.* 'Castaliiflora', impossible to distinguish until the buds open. The bright-yellow stamens are tipped with blue, and the light-green leaves are occasionally splashed with brown above and flushed with rose beneath. Pring, 1917. (1½-2½ ft (45-75 cm)).

'Imperial' (*N.* 'August Koch' X *N. coerulea*). This is a compact hybrid with gorgeous, rich-purple blossoms and a delicious fragrance. Beldt. (1½-2½ ft (45-75 cm)).

'Independence', *N.* 'Mrs Robert Sawyer'. The flowers are a rich rose-pink, and the foliage green with a reddish infusion. It is strongly viviparous and a good tub plant. Tricker, 1927. (1½-2½ ft (45-75 cm)).

'Isabelle Pring' The fragrant, globular, white blooms display golden stamens, and the large, light-green leaves with reddish undersides fade to green with age. It is viviparous. Pring, 1941. (1½-2½ ft (45-75 cm)).

'Jack Wood' This recent introduction has fragrant, rich raspberry-coloured blossoms with golden centres, and the leaves are green flecked with brown. Wood. (1½-2½ ft (45-75 cm)).

'Jamie Lu Skare' The fragrant, intense-yellow, star-shaped blossoms are borne on strong stems. Van Ness Nurseries, 1970. (1½-2½ ft (45-75 cm)).

'Janice' This small-growing variety has attractive, white, almost campanulate flowers which age to pale blue, and it is strongly viviparous. Tricker, 1928. (1-1½ ft (30-45 cm)).

'Joe Cutak' The medium-sized, soft-blue flowers have bright yellow centres. The foliage is green flecked with brown. Pring. (1½-2½ ft (45-75 cm)).

'Judge Hitchcock' The broad, cup-shaped blooms of purplish-blue intensify to violet towards the tips of the petals, and there are numerous golden stamens with purple anthers. The small, dark-green. leaves are flecked with brown, purplish beneath. Pring, 1941. (1½-2½ ft (45-75 cm)).

'King of the Blues' The dark-blue, velvety flowers have golden stamens that are tipped with blue, and the sepals are blue, overlaid maroon. Slocum, 1955. (1½-2½ ft (45-75 cm)).

'L. Dittmann' (*N. capensis* X *N. gigantea*?). This vigorous, rose-pink variety is currently scarce or lost to cultivation. Henkel, 1902. (1½-2½ ft (45-75 cm)).

'Leading Lady' This very fragrant, almost semi-double variety, bears huge, peach-coloured blossoms that open flat, and are held above large, deep-green, scalloped leaves with a distinctive brown freckling. The flowers will remain open under artificial light. Randig, 1938. (2½-3½ ft (75 cm-1 m)).

'Leopardess' The fragrant, medium-sized, cobalt-blue flowers are held above dark-green leaves that are heavily blotched with chocolate. Randig, 1931. (1½-2½ ft (45-75 cm)).

'Lindy' See *N.* 'Colonel Lindberg'.

'Listeri' This bears rich-blue, stellate flowers, but is scarce in cultivation. 1911. (1½-2½ ft (45-75 cm)).

'Lord Brooke' This is the pink version of *N.* 'Listeri'. 1911. (1½-2½ ft (45-75 cm)).

'Los Angeles' This has soft-pink, stellate flowers and attractive, mottled foliage. (1½-2½ ft (45-75 cm)).

'Louella G. Uber' This pure-white version of *N.* 'Leading Lady' is very fragrant. Van Ness Nurseries, 1970. (2½-3½ ft (75 cm-1 m)).

'Madame Abel Chatney' The pale-lavender flowers are held above striking mottled foliage. Lagrange, 1908. (1½-2½ ft (45-75 cm)).

'Madame Herbert Cutbush' The long, tapering flowers are of a smoky-blue. Lagrange. (1½-2 ft (45-60 cm)).

Madame Le Page Viger' The soft blush-pink blooms have red margins to the petals. Lagrange. (1½-2½ ft (45-75 cm)).

'Margaret Mary' This is an excellent miniature blue variety for tub or aquarium culture. The tiny, stellate blossoms, no more than an inch (25 mm) across, sport golden stamens. The leaves are 2 or 3 in (5-8 cm) across, dark green above, light brown beneath. It will flower all the year round if given warmth, but really needs a brief resting period every three or four months in order to recuperate. This is one of the most important developments in waterlily hybrids in recent years, and is viviparous. Plant patent No. 24533, 17 November 1964. Thomas. (1 ft (30 cm)).

'Margaret Randig' The large, somewhat flat, dark-blue blossoms with numerous broad petals have a delicious fragrance. The dark-green leaves are speckled with bronze, and it is very vigorous. Randig, 1939. (1½-3½ ft (45 cm-1 m)).

'Marmorata' See *N.* 'Mrs Edwards Whitaker' Marmorate form.

'Maynardii' The medium-sized flowers are of a pale violet-blue. (1½-2½ ft (45-75 cm)).

'Micheliana' This produces medium-sized, rosy-lilac blooms. (1½-2½ ft (45-75 cm)).

'Midnight' (*N. capensis* var. *zanzibariensis* 'Jupiter' X *N. colorata*). This is a curious variety with its small, rich-purple flowers consisting of several large, broad, outer petals and a cluster of small, modified petals around a tiny, golden centre. It is deliciously scented. The small, dark-green leaves are flecked with brown, deep purple beneath. Pring, 1941. (1-2 ft (30-60 cm)).

'Mr Martin E. Randig' The attractive blossoms of soft magenta have long tapering petals; the leaves are deep green, lightly blotched and with a reddish infusion beneath. (1½-2½ ft (45-75 cm)).

'Mrs Edwards Whitaker' (*N.* 'Castaliiflora' X *N. ovalifolia*). The large, lavender-blue flowers are up to a foot (30 cm) across and fade to a silvery-white with age. The petals are thin and papery, and the stamens bright yellow. The leaves are more-or-less orbicular with slightly undulating margins, dark green rarely spotted with brownish-green at the base; the undersides are light green with purplish-blue spots. Pring, 1917. (1½-3½ ft (45 cm-1 m)).

'Mrs Edwards Whitaker' Marmorate Form. *N.* 'Marmorata'. The flowers are cup-shaped, smaller and darker than the type, and the leaves light green, irregularly blotched with reddish-brown. It is believed to be a mutation from the original cross. Pring, 1917. (1½-3½ ft (45 cm-1 m)).

'Mrs George H. Pring', *N.* 'White Star'. (*N.* 'Mrs Edwards Whitaker' X *N. ovalifolia*). Silver Medal of the Society of American Florists, 1922. The very fragrant, stellate, creamy-white flowers are up to 10 in (25 cm) across, and the stamens are yellow with white tips. The large, green leaves are occasionally daubed with reddish-brown and have purplish reverses. Pring, 1922. (1½-2½ ft (45-75 cm)).

'Mrs Martin E. Randig' The fragrant, dark-purple blossoms have dark rose-pink sepals. The green leaves have reddish undersides and the plant is viviparous. Plant patent No. 294, 11 October 1938. Randig. (1½-2½ ft (45-75 cm)).

'Mrs Robert Sawyer' See *N.* 'Independence'.

'Mrs Woodrow Wilson' The thick-petalled flowers are of lavender-blue, and the yellow stamens are tipped with blue. The more-or-less heart-shaped, dark-green leaves have occasional splashes of brown. It is strongly viviparous. Tricker. (1½-2½ ft (45-75 cm)).

'Mrs Woodrow Wilson Gigantea' (*N.* 'Castaliiflora' X *N.* 'Mrs Woodrow Wilson'). The large, mid-blue, highly fragrant blossoms are borne on strong, tall peduncles. The small, dark-green leaves are spotted with brown, with brownish-pink undersides. Pring, 1917. (1½-2½ ft (45-75 cm)).

'Mrs W.R. James' (*N*. 'Mrs Edwards Whitaker' X *N*. 'Castaliiflora') The huge, very fragrant, deep-pink flowers with pale-pink sepals are held well above the surface of the water. The leaves are olive-green with brownish undersides. Koch, 1930. (1½-3½ ft (45 cm-1m)).

'Noelene' This gorgeous lavender hybrid has heavily mottled leaves. It was introduced to the United States from Australia in 1973, but apparently not yet into Great Britain. (1½-2½ ft (45-75 cm)).

'Pamela' The beautiful, large, sky-blue flowers up to a foot (30 cm) across are held well above the water. The leaves are green with a brown mottling. Koch, 1931. (1½-2½ ft (45-75 cm)).

'Panama Pacific' The buds open a purplish-blue, but turn to rich reddish-purple when the blossoms are expanded. The golden stamens have violet anthers, and the buds are bronze-green spotted with brown. The leaves are bronze-green with reddish veins. This strongly viviparous hybrid is one of the hardier tropicals. Tricker, 1914. (1½-2½ ft (45-75 cm)).

'Patricia' This is a small-growing, almost pygmy, crimson variety with small, pale-green leaves. It is viviparous, and is ideal for tub culture. Tricker. (1-1½ ft (30-45 cm)).

'Peach Blow' The large, rounded, deep-pink flowers lighten towards the centre, and the light-green leaves are lightly flecked with red. It is strongly viviparous. (1½-2½ ft (45-75 cm)).

'Pearl Sensation' This delicate, pink hybrid is little known in Great Britain. (1½-2½ ft (45-75 cm)).

'Pennsylvania' See *N*. 'Blue Beauty'.

'Persian Lilac' This produces large, fragrant, broad-petalled, pink flowers with golden stamens and pink anthers. The small green leaves have occasional brownish flecks, and are crimson on the undersides. Pring, 1941. (1½-2½ ft (45-75 cm)).

'Pink Delight' The blooms are free-flowering and rose-carmine in colour. Johnson, 1934. (1½-2½ ft (45-75 cm)).

'Pink Pearl' The fragrant flowers of bright, silvery pink with pure-white throats and yellow stamens are held high above the water. The leaves are green and reddish-brown beneath. Koch. (1½-2½ ft (45-75 cm)).

'Pink Perfection' The fragrant, deep-pink blossoms display numerous yellow stamens tipped with pink. The leaves are green and heavily mottled with reddish-brown. Lingg. (1½-2½ ft (45-75 cm)).

'Pink Platter' This has broad, open blooms consisting of numerous, long, narrow, soft-pink petals, and the stamens are golden and pink. The large, light-green leaves are liberally splashed with chestnut-brown. It is viviparous. (1½-2½ ft (45-75 cm)).

'Pocahontas' This is a larger version of *N*. 'Pink Pearl'. (1½-3½ ft

(45 cm-1 m)).

'Pride of Winter Haven' Very compact and free-flowering, this hybrid bears rich fuchsia-lavender, stellate blossoms. Slocum, 1977. (1½-2½ ft (45-75 cm)).

'Pulcherrima' See *N*. 'Blue Beauty'.

'Radiant Red' This is a deep-red hybrid. (1½-2½ ft (45-75 cm)).

'Red Beauty' This exceptional hybrid is a deep red. Slocum, 1966. (1½-2½ ft (45-75 cm)).

'Red Blaze' The prolific, medium-sized, light-red blossoms have deep orange centres. (1½-2½ ft (45-75 cm)).

'Reine d'Italie' The deep-purple blossoms have bright-red stamens. (1½-2½ ft (45-75 cm)).

'Rio Rita' The spreading blooms have broad petals of glowing amaranth-pink and purplish stamens. The small green leaves are flecked with brown and have reddish undersides. Pring, 1941. (1½-2½ ft (45-75 cm)).

'Rose Pearl' This produces large, full, deep rose-pink flowers. Wood. (1½-2½ ft (45-75 cm)).

'Royal(e) Purple' The thick, velvety-petalled flowers are deep purple with contrasting golden sepals. It is viviparous and good for tub culture. Buskirk. (1½-2½ ft (45-75 cm)).

'St Louis' (*N*. 'Mrs George H. Pring' X *N. burtii*). Henry Shaw Gold Medal, 1933. The large, stellate, canary-yellow blossoms display yellow stamens. The pea-green leaves are faintly spotted with brown when young. Plant patent No. 55, 28 February 1933. Pring, 1932. (1½-2½ ft (45-75 cm)).

'St Louis Gold' The medium-sized blossoms are a citron-yellow, and the leaves are dark green flushed with brown, which disappears with age. This is an excellent tub plant. Pring. (1½-2½ ft (45-75 cm)).

'St Louis' Marmorate Form. This is as *N*. 'St. Louis', but with petals fading to pink. The buds are striped with purple and the leaves heavily mottled with maroon. Pring, 1932. (1½-2½ ft (45-75 cm)).

'Shell Pink' The clear, pink, bowl-like blooms have golden stamens. The large, green leaves are flecked with brown, with the undersides pinkish. It is viviparous. Pring, 1934. (1½-2½ ft (45-75 cm)).

'Shirley Ann' This blue hybrid is thought to be lost to cultivation. Tricker. (1½-2½ ft (45-75 cm)).

'Shirley Marie' This vigorous waterlily, with its huge, deep-pink blossoms, was developed by the New York Botanical Gardens. (1½-3½ ft (45 cm-1 m)).

'Snow White' The pure-white, cup-shaped blossoms are held well above the water, and it is a good cut-flower variety. Beldt. (1½-2½ ft (45-75 cm)).

'Sunbeam' This looks very much like *N*. 'St. Louis' when the buds first open, but becomes dark golden-yellow with age. The young buds are striped with purple before opening, and the light-green leaves are flushed with purple and have pinkish undersides. It is viviparous. Pring. (1½-2½ ft (45-75 cm)).

'Talisman' The large, star-like flowers of pale primrose are heavily overlaid with bright pink. The small, dark-green leaves are flecked with purplish-brown when young. The plant is strongly viviparous. Pring, 1941. (1½-2½ ft (45-75 cm)).

'Tammie Sue Uber' The beautiful, very fragrant, deep-rose blossoms have long, tapering petals. Van Ness Nurseries, 1970. (1½-2½ ft (45-75 cm)).

'Tanganyika' This name is used in the trade for the selection of *N. heudelotii* formerly referred to as *N. guineensis*. See *N. heudelotii*.

'Ted Uber' The large, fragrant, semi-double, white blossoms with their bright-yellow centres are held above the surface of the water. The deep-green leaves have a pink flush and the plant is vigorous. (1½-3½ ft (45 cm-1 m)).

'Tina' This multi-coloured, viviparous hybrid combines shades of blue and pink, and the bright-yellow centre is surrounded with lavender stamens. Van Ness Nurseries. (1½-2½ ft (45-75 cm)).

'Trailblazer' This hybrid has fragrant, deep-yellow, stellate blooms and handsome, fresh-green foliage with purplish undersides. Randig, 1938. (1½-2½ ft (45-75 cm)).

'Virginia Grossi' The medium-sized flowers are smoky-blue. (1½-2½ ft (45-75 cm)).

'Violet' This produces very fragrant, violet-blue blossoms and undulating leaves. (1½-2½ ft (45-75 cm)).

'White Star' See *N.* 'Mrs George H. Pring'.

'Wild Rose' The bright-pink blooms have large, velvety petals and golden stamens with pinkish anthers. The dark-green leaves are flecked with brown, and are reddish beneath. It is viviparous. Pring, 1941. (1½-2½ ft (45-75 cm)).

'William C. Uber' This strong-growing hybrid has fragrant, deep-rose flowers and large, fresh-green leaves. Van Ness Nurseries, 1970. (1½-3½ ft (45 cm-1 m)).

'William T. Innes' (*N.* 'Mrs George H. Pring' X *N. capensis* var. *zanzibariensis* f. *rosea*). This has pale-blue, medium-sized blossoms and green leaves speckled with chocolate. Beldt, 1944. (1½-2½ ft (45-75 cm)).

'William Ward' This is a large, carmine-rose hybrid said to be derived from *N. capensis* var. *zanzibariensis* and should possibly be grouped under that section. (1½-2½ ft (45-75 cm)).

'Yellow Dazzler' This is an outstanding yellow variety. The huge, flat, lemon, star-like blooms, which are carried on stems some 6 in (15 cm) above the water, are produced in abundance throughout the summer. The foliage is plain green and of enormous proportions. Randig, 1938. (1½-3½ ft (45 cm-1 m)).

'Yellow Mystery' The yellow blossoms have petals tipped with pale blue, and the deep-green leaves have purplish undersides. (1½-2½ ft (45-75 cm)).

'Yellow Star' The stellate blooms with their long, tapering, bright-yellow petals are held high above the water. It has large, plain-green leaves. Pring, 1922. (1½-2½ ft (45-75 cm)).

CHAPTER 8

Tropical, Night-blooming Hybrids

'Adele', *N. ortigiesiana* var. *adele*. The medium-sized carmine blossoms have narrow pointed petals, green sepals and bright-yellow stamens. It is extremely scarce in cultivation. *C.* 1888. (1½-2½ ft (45-75 cm)).

'Albert d'Argence' The red blossoms have bright, reddish-orange stamens. (1½-2½ ft (45-75 cm)).

'Antares' (*Nymphaea* 'H.C. Haarstick' X *N.* 'Emily Grant Hutchings'). The cup-shaped blossoms are 6 to 8 in (15-20 cm) across and of a deep-purple colour. The irregular, toothed green leaves have a purplish infusion. Longwood Gardens, Pennsylvania, 1962. (1½-2½ ft (45-75 cm)).

'Armand Millet' The huge, brilliant wine-red flowers are borne above dark-green, serrated leaves. (1½-2½ ft (45-75 cm)).

'Arnoldiana' (*N. rubra* X *N. lotus* var. *dentata*). This produces attractive carmine blossoms. Oliver, *c.* 1900. (1½-2½ ft (45-75 cm)).

'B.C. Berry' The large, shallow flowers of amaranth-purple shade lighter towards the centre. The medium-sized, dark-green leaves have a faint purplish mottling and indented margins. (1½-2½ ft (45-75 cm)).

'Bissetii' (*N.* 'Sturtevantii X *N. lotus* var. *dentata*?). The fully double, cup-shaped blooms of glowing rose-pink are held well above the water. The bronze-green leaves have serrated margins. (1½-2½ ft (45-75 cm)).

'Boucheana' (*N. rubra* X *N. lotus* var. *dentata*). The large, open flowers have broad, rose-pink petals and yellow stamens, and the leaves are a rich green. This hybrid is sterile. Bouche, 1853. (1½-2½ ft (45-75 cm)).

'C.E. Hutchings' The cup-shaped blossoms are of bright red with crimson centres, and the dark-green foliage is infused with bronze. (1½-2½ ft (45-75 cm)).

'Charles L. Tricker' This very free-flowering, red hybrid has dark reddish-green leaves. (1½-2½ ft (45-75 cm)).

'Columbiana' The deep-crimson, stellate blooms are up to 6 in (15 cm) in diameter, and the foliage is a dark reddish-green. Tricker, 1894. (1½-2½ ft (45-75 cm)).

'Deaniana' (Sometimes called *N.* 'Dean'). (*N.* 'Boucheana' X *N.* 'Indica Spira'?). The shallow, clear, pink, cup-shaped flowers have golden stamens. The bronze-green foliage is large, the individual pads being up to 18 in (45 cm) across. Tricker. (1½-2½ ft (45-75 cm)).

'Delicatissima', *N. lotus* 'Delicata'. (*N. lotus* var. *dentata* X *N. rubra*). This has pale, almost flesh-pink flowers and undulating, glaucous foliage. Tricker, 1894. (1½-2½ ft (45-75 cm)).

'Devoniensis' (Sometimes called 'Devon' or 'Devonshire'). This seedling from *N. rubra* was originally believed to be a *N. rubra* X *N. lotus* hybrid. The immense, brilliant-red flowers up to a foot (30 cm) across, and with rich-red stamens, are held above handsome, bronze-green foliage. Paxton, 1851. (2-3 ft (60-90 cm)).

'Diana' (*N.* 'Sturtevantii' X *N. amazonum*). The slightly fragrant, intense rose-pink blooms are infused with red, the stamens are brown with a pinkish flush and the sepals are red, with a greenish infusion. The orbicular, deeply cleft leaves are a foot (30 cm) or so across, the upper surfaces being a deep brownish-green and purplish beneath. Certificate of Merit, Massachusetts Horticultural Society, 21 July 1900. Grey, 1900. (1½-2½ ft (45-75 cm)).

'Diana Grandiflora' This is a larger-flowered version of *N.* 'Diana' and of a deeper red. The larger leaves, up to 18 in (45 cm) across, have slightly pubescent undersides. Grey. (1½-3 ft (45-90 cm)).

'Doctor Florenze' This bears medium-sized, blood-red blossoms and expansive leaves. It is very rare, if not lost to cultivation. (1½-2½ ft (45-75 cm)).

'Eastonensis' (*N.* 'Omarana' X *N.* 'Smithiana'). The white flowers are shaded with steely-blue, and have green sepals flushed with crimson. The orbicular foliage is dark green above and purple beneath. Ames, 1900. (1½-2½ ft (45-75 cm)).

'Emily Grant Hutchings' The large, deep pinkish-red, cup-shaped blooms with their deep amaranth stamens become rich mahogany with age, while the sepals and foliage have a bronzed-crimson overlay. The individual leaves are relatively small with undulating margins. It was raised by George Pring and named after the wife of the secretary of Tower Grove Park, in which the Missouri Botanical Garden is situated. 1922. (1½-2½ ft (45-75 cm)).

'Frank Trelease' (*N.* 'Devoniensis' X *N.* 'Omarana'). The deep-crimson blooms have long, narrow petals and bright-red stamens. The dark coppery leaves are splashed with green beneath. Gurney, 1900. (1½-2½ ft (45-75 cm)).

'George Huster' (*N.* 'Omarana' X *N. rubra*). The large, stellate, rich velvety-red flowers are held 6 in (15 cm) above the surface of the water, and the circular, bronze-green leaves have crinkled edges. Dreer, 1899. (1½-2½ ft (45-75 cm)).

'H.C. Haarstick' The enormous, brilliant-red blossoms with their long, tapering petals display red and gold stamens, and the large, coppery leaves have indented margins. Some authorities consider this to be a variety of *N. zenkeri*. 1922. (1½-3½ ft (45 cm-1 m)).

'Indica' (*N. rubra* X *N. lotus*). Various forms of this union have been named, and come under the general heading of *N.* 'Indica'. The blossoms of the true form are 5 or 6 in (13 or 15 cm) in diameter, pure white and fragrant. (1½-2½ ft (45-75 cm)).

'Indica Brahma' This produces flaming-red blossoms. (1½-2½ ft (45-75 cm)).

'Indica Hofgarten Direktor Graebner' The inward-curving, deep-rose blooms intensify towards the centre, and the large, deeply serrated foliage is reddish. (1½-2½ ft (45-75 cm)).

'Indica Isis' The rounded blooms are of a delicate pale pink. (1½-2½ ft (45-75 cm)).

'Indica Spira' This has large, globular, rose-pink blossoms. Moenkemeyer, 1897. (1½-2½ ft (45-75 cm)).

'James Gurney Jr' The fragrant, deep rose-pink flowers with their orange stamens are held well above the water. The leaves are large, reddish-green, and purplish beneath. Pring, 1948. (1½-2½ ft (45-75 cm)).

'Janice Ruth' This is a hybrid of moderate growth, producing pure-white blooms with yellow centres. The leaves are dark green. (1-1½ ft (30-45 cm)).

'Jubilee' The pure-white flowers are up to 9 in (23 cm) across with pinkish sepals and pale-pink bases to the outer petals. The broad, deeply dentate foliage is green blotched with brown. Dreer, 1899. (1½-2½ ft (45-75 cm)).

'Jules Vacherot' The brilliant-red blooms are produced in abundance. Lagrange. (1½-2½ ft (45-75 cm)).

'Kewensis' (*N. lotus* var. *dentata* X *N.* 'Devoniensis'). The soft rose-pink flowers with their light-green sepals lie flat on the surface of the water. The leaves are rounded, dark green blotched with brown above and purplish beneath. Watson, 1885. Once lost to cultivation, this hybrid was re-established by Dreer in 1900. (1½-2½ ft (45-75 cm)).

'Krumbiegelii' This is free-flowering and a deep carmine-red. (1½-2½ ft (45-75 cm)).

'Iverney' This hybrid produces large, purplish-pink, stellate blossoms. (1½-2½ ft (45-75 cm)).

'La Reine de Los Angeles' The full, broad-petalled flowers of pure white have central clusters of golden stamens. Johnson, 1935. (1½-2½ ft (45-75 cm)).

'Laelia' (*N.* 'Columbiana' X *N.* 'Smithiana'). The almond-scented blossoms are a delicate, pale rose-pink. The ovate foliage is green above and purplish beneath, with hairy petioles. (1½-2½ ft (45-75 cm)).

'Laelia Colorans' This compact variant has smaller, more deeply coloured flowers. (1-2 ft (30-60 cm)).

'Madame Auguste Tezier' The lavender-blue flowers intensify to violet at the centre, and display nut-brown stamens. The handsome, purple, dentate foliage is splashed and spotted with brown. Lagrange, 1914. (1½-2½ ft (45-75 cm)).

'Marie Lagrange' (*N. lotus* X *N. lotus* var. *dentata*). The deep rosy-purple blooms have a conspicuous white line running down the centre of each petal, and the stamens are a golden-yellow. Lagrange, *c.* 1899. (1½-2½ ft (45-75 cm)).

'Maroon Beauty' This is a free-flowering selection with deep maroon blossoms. Slocum, 1950. (1½-2½ ft (45-75 cm)).

'Mars' The blooms are a glowing rosy-vermilion. Johnson, 1933. (1½-2½ ft (45-75 cm)).

'Minerva' This produces huge, white, cup-shaped blooms and dark olive-green foliage. (1½-2½ ft (45-75 cm)).

'Missouri' (*N.* 'Mrs George C. Hitchcock' X *N.* 'Sturtevantii'?). The immense flowers up to 15 in (38 cm) across are of the purest white and held high above the water on thick, succulent flower stems. The petals are broad, and surround a central boss of erect stamens. The dark-green leaves have indented margins and are strikingly mottled with purple and brown. Pring, 1932. (2½-3½ ft (75 cm-1 m).

'Mrs John A. Wood' This recent introduction has maroon-red, stellate blossoms and reddish-purple foliage. Wood. (1½-2½ ft (45-75 cm)).

'Mrs George C. Hitchcock' (*N.* 'Omarana' X *N.* 'Omarana'). The large, rose-pink blooms display conspicuous, orange stamens, and the coppery-green foliage has undulating margins and purplish reverses. Pring, 1926. (1½-2½ ft (45-75 cm)).

'Niobe' (*N. amazonum* X *N. rubra*). This bears medium-sized, magenta blossoms with a sweet fragrance of almonds which are held well above the surface of the water. The sepals are green infused with pink, and the stamens pink with brownish anthers. The orbicular, toothed leaves are dark patchy-green above, purplish-brown beneath and have pubescent veins and petioles. Ames, 1900. (1½-2½ ft (45-75 cm)).

'Omarana' (*N. lotus* var. *dentata* X *N.* 'Sturtevantii'). The pale-pink blooms intensify to rose-pink at their centre, and there is a faint, white line running down the centre of each petal surrounding the central boss of fiery-orange stamens. The plain-green leaves have wavy margins. It is very vigorous. Bisset, 1894. (1½-3½ ft (45 cm-1 m)).

'Ortgiesiana Alba' *N. ortgiesiana* is a synonym of *N. lotus*, but this hybrid, although bearing the '*ortgiesiana*' name, is thought not to be derived solely from that species and cannot be properly accommodated within it. It has no alternative synonym, and therefore must stand alone, for the time being at least. The large, spreading blooms are a soft creamy-white with purple centres, and the sepals are striped with green. Ortgies. (1½-2½ ft (45-75 cm)).

'Ortgiesiana Rubra' (*N. lotus* X *N. rubra*?). This produces rose-pink blossoms and dark-green, rounded leaves with toothed margins. Ortgies, 1852. (1½-2½ ft (45-75 cm)).

'President Girard' The medium-sized blooms are a carmine-rose. (1½-2½ ft (45-75 cm)).

'Pride of California' The deep-red, stellate flowers are held high above the water, and the leaves are coppery-green. Johnson, 1935. (1½-2½ ft (45-75 cm)).

'Purpurea' (Sometimes called *N.* 'Purpuralis'). The small, rather pointed blooms are of a deep purplish-red. (1-1½ ft (30-45 cm)).

'Queen Elizabeth' (*N. ortgiesiana* X *N.* 'Devoniensis'). This has bright-red, stellate blossoms. (1½-2½ ft (45-75 cm)).

'Red Flare' This has fragrant, intense-red, stellate blossoms and deep mahogany foliage. Randig, 1938. (1½-2½ ft (45-75 cm)).

'Rosa de Nocha' The creamy-white blossoms shade to pink at the tips of the petals, and have bright-yellow centres. The leaves are large, and of a bright reddish-green. (1½-2½ ft (45-75 cm)).

'Rubicunda' (*N.* 'Sturtevantii' X *N. lotus*). The large, pink blossoms shade to white in the centre, and the sepals are green, with a pink infusion. The large, circular, toothed leaves are 12 in (30 cm) across, and the petioles green, with purplish spots. Ames, 1900. (1½-2½ ft (45-75 cm)).

'Rufus J. Lackland' The large, intense-crimson flowers age to deep plum. Gurney. (1½-2½ ft (45-75 cm)).

'Sir Galahad' This strong-growing variety has immense, green, undulating leaves, striking stellate blossoms of cool icy-white and yellow stamens. Randig. (1½-3 ft (45-90 cm)).

'Smithiana' The medium-sized, cup-shaped, creamy-white blooms have golden stamens, and the leaves are dark green. Tricker, 1893. (1½-2½ ft (45-75 cm)).

'Sturtevantii' (*N. lotus* X *N.* 'Devoniensis') The large, deliciously scented, stellate blossoms of iridescent-pink are held well above the water, and the wavy, reddish foliage ages to coppery-green. It needs a temperature of at least 80°F (27°C) to grow successfully. Sturtevant, 1884. (1½-2½ ft (45-75 cm)).

'Trickeri' (*N. lotus* var. *dentata* X *N.* 'Sturtevantii'). The light rose-pink blossoms are shaded with white, and the large, toothed leaves have prominent veins, and are green above, brown beneath. Tricker, 1893. (1½-2½ ft (45-75 cm)).

'Trudy Slocum' This prolific, white-flowered hybrid displays a prominent cluster of golden stamens. The foliage is plain green. Slocum, 1948. (1½-2½ ft (45-75 cm)).

'Wood's White Knight' (*N.* 'Sir Galahad' X *N.* 'Missouri'). The beautiful creamy-white blossoms have prominent golden stamens. The leaves are green, with a darker dappling beneath. Wood. (1½-2½ ft (45-75 cm)).

CHAPTER 9

Hybridisation

With most genera of plants the means by which new hybrids were derived, together with their parentage, is often a mystery. An aura of secrecy surrounds the methods used by their creators, either because of commercial considerations, personal pride, or else to create a mystical climate conducive to engendering public interest in the new and wonderful hybrid being launched on the market.

Waterlilies have suffered more than most from this kind of treatment, the most important and successful hybridiser, Latour-Marliac, taking the secrets of his life's work to his grave. From reports of the time it would appear that he was not only evasive about his techniques and the parentage of his hybrids, but on occasions tried to throw enquirers off the scent by giving dubious information. However, despite his shortcomings as a mentor, it cannot be disputed that he was the greatest waterlily hybridiser the world has known.

The achievements of other hybridisers in the hardy-waterlily field have been negligible compared with those of Marliac. Indeed, Frances Perry, one of the most important authorities on aquatic plants in Great Britain and daughter-in-law of probably the most successful raiser of new varieties in this country, the late Amos Perry, stated in her authoritative work on water gardening

> The hybridization of waterlilies is generally so much fruitless labour, and the results far from encouraging. Out of 159 recorded crosses we made in 1927, only one pod set seed, and the offspring was no better, and indeed, not as good as many of the existing varieties.

In fact, if one studies the achievements of various introducers of new hardy cultivars, it will be discovered that in a good number of cases these are selected forms or improved seedlings of a species rather than a direct cross between two distinct parents.

With tropical waterlilies we are a little more fortunate, for the most successful hybridiser, George Pring of the Missouri Botanical

Garden, St Louis, kept records of his work and divulged freely of his successes and failures. For those whose interest is more academic, the details of his work are shown on pages 91-101. The early successes at raising new varieties are enumerated, together with the 246 pollinations made with *Nymphaea burttii* after its introduction in 1929. My grateful thanks for this information go to Stephen Wolff of the Missouri Botanical Garden, who has gone to great trouble to see that I have had as much detail as possible of George Pring's work at my fingertips.

George Pring began experimenting with tropical waterlilies in 1915, with the intention of producing a white hybrid of good size and form. He was assisted in his quest by Peter Bisset's introduction of seed from Africa of *N. ovalifolia*, and the subsequent successful rearing of seedlings by E.T. Harvey of Cincinnati. *N. ovalifolia* is a vigorous grower, with large, white flowers tipped with blue, but unfortunately has far fewer petals than is horticulturally desirable. *N. ovalifolia* was then crossed with *N.* 'Castaliiflora' (a hybrid made by George Pring in 1912 between two light-pink forms of *N. capensis* var. *zanzibariensis*). The resulting seeds germinated freely, and produced a plant with large, blue flowers which aged to off-white. This was *N.* 'Mrs Edwards Whitaker'.

Using *N.* 'Mrs Edwards Whitaker' as a staminate parent and *N. ovalifolia* as a pistillate parent, blue-flowered plants were produced. However, a reciprocal cross resulted in white becoming the dominant colour. The best white form showing the typical flower and leaf characteristics of *N.* 'Mrs Edwards Whitaker' was selected, and during the summers of 1920 and 1921 was self-pollinated, its progeny producing white flowers. The best of these were reselected and self-pollinated, and gave rise to plants with blossoms of increased size and with more numerous petals. Continued selection to eliminate those with infusions of pink or blue was carried on until the desirable white form was fixed. This was achieved in 1922 and named *N.* 'Mrs George H. Pring'.

The interesting thing about *N.* 'Mrs George H. Pring' is that its parentage was dominantly blue. Previously *N. flavo-virens*, a pure white Mexican species, had been hybridised with various forms of *N. capensis* var. *zanzibariensis*, but in the resulting seedlings white was recessive, and the hybrids thus yielded, like *N.* 'Mrs C.W. Ward' and *N.* 'William Stope', possessed the stellate blossoms of *N. flavo-virens*.

In 1929 the introduction of the yellow-flowered *N. burttii* from Tanganyika provided George Pring with additional valuable material. In 1930 he made 86 crosses with *N. burttii*. One between *N. burttii* and *N.* 'Independence' produced seedlings with pink and blue dominant and yellow recessive, but all of viviparous habit. The pale blue of the second generation, when selfed, produced yellow as the dominant colour, but with the dark blues and pinks, yellow was again recessive. The original cross made with *N. burttii* as the staminate parent yielded the pale-blue colour, and in the second generation showed yellow dominant. However, when *N.* 'Independence' was the staminate parent, blue and pink were always dominant. Only when *N. burttii* was crossed with a white such as *N.* 'Mrs George H. Pring' was yellow dominant and all the other colours recessive. Curiously when crossed with the white *N. ovalifolia*, yellow and blue proved dominant and pink and white recessive. Subsequently amidst these complexities George Pring produced a fixed yellow of outstanding merit and called it *N.* 'St Louis'.

This then is an outline of the important landmarks and discoveries in George Pring's work. He, and latterly other hybridisers like Martin Randig and Perry Slocum have built on this knowledge and developed some truly wonderful cultivars. Of course, it must not be thought that George Pring alone forged the way ahead for modern tropical waterlily hybrids, for sterling work was performed by E. Sturtevant, William Tricker and Peter Bisset in earlier years. However, it must be said that George Pring made the important colour breaks and kept the best-documented breeding programme, and for this he deserves due credit.

From the multiplicity of cultivars available one might suppose that waterlily hybridising has outlived its usefulness, but there are still mountains to climb, particularly with the hardy varieties, where the gorgeous blues of the tropicals are totally lacking. Who will take up the challenge is difficult to say, for space and capital are necessary to implement a comprehensive breeding programme. The keen hobbyist can make a contribution though, if he has the inclination. An average-sized, prefabricated pool and a tub or two will hold a surprising amount of material. For those interested in pursuing this further, the following short account of pollination and seed collection may be of some value.

The blossom selected for seed production must be protected from insect pollination and emasculated in order to ensure a pure cross. This must be done in the late bud stage, and involves removing the stamens in order to prevent self-pollination. The experts use forceps, but pointed scissors are usually quite adequate. Both scissors and fingers should be sterilised in methylated spirits before starting emasculation, and as often as different varieties are handled. This should be wiped off or allowed to evaporate before emasculating, otherwise the delicate surface of the stigma may be damaged.

Emasculation should be performed as late as possible before the anthers erupt, and if perchance they burst during the operation then the entire flower should be discarded. In order to remove the stamens it is generally acknowledged that a number, if not all the petals should be removed. I find this unnecessary in the majority of cases and prefer to leave the flower intact, as without the protection of the petals the delicate styles may dry up. Also, by preventing the various portions of the flower from fulfilling their natural functions, premature detachment of the flower stalk is likely.

On the first day of opening the centre of the prepared flower will be full of nectar. It is at this time that pollination must take place. This involves taking the anthers containing pollen from the chosen male donor and placing it on the pistil of the selected seed parent. The process having been completed, the entire bloom should be enclosed in a muslin bag to exclude the attentions of insects. George Pring recommended that a string be attached to the flower stem and secured to a stake near the crown of the plant to assist with easy inspection of the developing seed pod, as with most kinds, once pollination has been successful, the old flower head closes tightly and thrusts itself down into the water in order to prevent the developing seeds drying out. Once the seed is ripe the pod will rise to the surface of the water, rupture, and scatter its seed. If the muslin bag is attached properly the seed will be retained and can be sown as recommended on page 120. To ensure that only viable seed is sown, float the contents of the bag in a jar of water. The seeds that fall to the bottom within five or six days will be the viable ones.

Finally, I must make an important point regarding the results likely to be achieved. In the first place a lot of mediocre material will result from an initial cross, and the majority of seedlings will have to be discarded. The second generation is where things may start to happen, but not necessarily the way one may expect. Initial selection from a first cross will probably mean the retention of seedlings with desirable characteristics, but it is one of the frustrations of plant breeding that a promising first-generation plant does not necessarily yield a better second-generation plant. Often the useful second-generation progeny is begat by a mediocre seedling from the first cross. Such is the frustration and fascination of hybridising.

The following are details of George Pring's early work, together with details of his hybridising work with *N. burttii*. Although this is not the complete documentation of his work — he also created fine cultivars from mutations (e.g. *N. tetragona* 'Johann Pring') — it serves as a useful indication of the amount of dedication involved in raising new varieties and of the unlikely results sometimes achieved. The first short list consists of cultivars raised and named by George Pring between 1913 and 1930. This gives no indication of the number of undesirable seedlings he must have discarded on his way to achieving his particular goals:

Nymphaea 'Castaliiflora'
  N. capensis var. *zanzibariensis* forma *rosea* X *N. capensis*
  var. *zanzibariensis* forma *rosea*
Nymphaea 'Mrs Edwards Whitaker 'Marmorate' Form
  N. 'Castaliiflora' X *N. ovalifolia*
Nymphaea 'General Pershing'
  N. 'Mrs Edwards Whitaker' X *N.* 'Castaliiflora'
Nymphaea 'Mrs Woodrow Wilson Gigantea'
  N. 'Castaliiflora' X *N.* 'Mrs Woodrow Wilson'
Nymphaea 'Henry Shaw'
  N. 'Castaliiflora' X *N.* 'Castaliiflora'
Nymphaea 'Mrs George H. Pring'
  N. 'Mrs Edwards Whitaker' X *N. ovalifolia*
Nymphaea 'Edward C. Eliot'
  N. 'Mrs Edwards Whitaker 'Marmorate' Form X *N.* 'Mrs. Edwards
  Whitaker 'Marmorate' Form

The pages following give the important record of crosses made by
George Pring using *N. burttii* and its progeny. The number of the
cross, date of pollination, the parents (female parent first), and the
fertility of the seed are given. In some cases only a few seeds were
found in seed-pods, in which case they are called 'fertile', although
often no germination resulted. The following abbreviations are used:

oval g. = *ovalifolia gigantea*
Koch = 'August P. Koch'
Pan. Pac. = 'Panama Pacific'
Whit. g. = 'Mrs Edwards
  Whitaker Gigantea'
Stone = 'William G. Stone'
Persh. = 'General Pershing'
Indep. = 'Independence'
Pring = 'Mrs George H. Pring'
Hitch. = 'Mrs George C.
  Hitchcock'
Sturtev. = 'Sturtevantii'

W. Wilson g. = 'Mrs Woodrow
  Wilson Gigantea'
Stella G. = 'Stella Gurney'
Shaw = 'Henry Shaw'
Hutch = 'Emily Grant Hutchings'
Haarst. = 'H.C. Haarstick'
Eliot = 'Edward C. Eliot'
Lotus g. = *lotus* var. *gigantea*
Pan. white = Undetermined
  white species from Panama
vivip. = viviparous

Date of cross	No.	Cross	Date of seed collection	Seed fertile	Seed sterile	
June 17	1	burttii X burttii	July 2		+	1930
Aug. 7	2	oval. g. X burttii	Aug. 25	+		
Aug. 7	3	Koch X burttii	Aug. 26		+	

Date of cross	No.	Cross	Date of seed collection	Seed fertile	Seed sterile
Aug. 7	4	Pan. Pac. X burttii	Aug. 26	+	
Aug. 7	5	Shaw X burttii	Sept. 2		+
Aug. 8	6	oval. g. X burttii	Aug. 25		+
Aug. 8	7	Koch X burttii	Aug. 30	+	
Aug. 8	8	Whit. g. X burttii	Aug. 26	+	
Aug. 11	9	oval. g. X burttii	Aug. 28		+
Aug. 11	10	Shaw X burttii	Sept. 2	+	
Aug. 11	11	Stone X burttii	Sept. 8	+	
Aug. 11	12	Persh. X burttii	Aug. 29		+
Aug. 11	13	Indep. X burttii	Sept. 8	+	
Aug. 11	14	Pring X burttii	Sept. 2	+	
Aug. 11	15	Stella G. X burttii	Sept. 2		+
Aug. 11	16	Lotus g. X burttii	Aug. 28		+
Aug. 12	17	oval. g. X burttii	Sept. 2		+
Aug. 12	18	Whit. g. X burttii	Aug. 27		+
Aug. 12	19	Koch X burttii	Aug. 27		+
Aug. 12	20	Lotus g. X burttii	Aug. 28		+
Aug. 12	21	Pring X burttii	Aug. 26		+
Aug. 12	22	Pring X burttii	Aug. 28		+
Aug. 13	23	burttii X burttii	Sept. 1		+
Aug. 13	24	Pan. Pac. X burttii	Aug. 28		+
Aug. 13	25	Persh. X burttii	Aug. 27		+
Aug. 13	26	Stone X burttii	Aug. 29		+
Aug. 14	27	Hitch. X Sturtev.	Sept. 5	+	
Aug. 16	28	Whit. g. X burttii	Sept. 4	+	
Aug. 16	29	Pan. Pac. X burttii	Sept. 8	+	
Aug. 16	30	Stella G. X burttii	Sept. 4		+
Aug. 16	31	Stella G. X burttii	Sept. 2		+
Aug. 16	32	Shaw X burttii	Aug. 31	+	
Aug. 16	33	Pring X burttii	Sept. 3		+
Aug. 16	34	Pring X burttii	Aug. 31		+
Aug. 16	35	Persh. X burttii	Sept. 3	+	
Aug. 16	36	Indep. X burttii	Sept. 3	+	
Aug. 16	37	Pring X burttii	Sept. 3	+	
Aug. 16	38	Koch X burttii	Sept. 8		+
Aug. 16	39	Shaw X burttii	Aug. 31		+
Aug. 16	40	Stone X burttii	Sept. 8	+	
Aug. 16	41	Whit. g. X burttii	Sept. 8	+	
Aug. 16	42	Whit. g. X burttii	Aug. 29		+

Date of cross	No.	Cross	Date of seed collection	Seed fertile	Seed sterile
Aug. 16	43	Indep. X burttii	Sept. 2	+	
Aug. 16	44	Pring X burttii	Sept. 2	+	
Aug. 18	45	Whit. g. X burttii	Sept. 3		+
Aug. 18	46	Persh. X burttii	Sept. 5		+
Aug. 18	47	Persh. X burttii	Sept. 2		+
Aug. 18	48	Koch X burttii	Sept. 5	+	
Aug. 18	49	Lotus g. X burttii	Aug. 29		+
Aug. 18	50	Stella G. X burttii	Sept. 4		+
Aug. 18	51	Stella G. X burttii	Sept. 4		+
Aug. 18	52	Stone X burttii	Sept. 2		+
Aug. 18	53	Pring X burttii	Sept. 6	+	
Aug. 18	54	burttii X burttii	Sept. 1		+
Aug. 19	55	burttii X burttii	Sept. 6	+	
Aug. 19	56	Indep. X burttii	Sept. 6		+
Aug. 19	57	Pring X burttii	Sept. 5	+	
Aug. 19	58	Stella G. X burttii	Sept. 3		+
Aug. 19	59	Stone X burttii	Sept. 14	+	
Aug. 20	60	Whit. g. X burttii	Sept. 8	+	
Aug. 20	61	Pan. Pac. X burttii	Sept. 6	+	
Aug. 20	62	Shaw X burttii	Sept. 5	+	
Aug. 20	63	Pring X burttii	Sept. 8	+	
Aug. 20	64	Indep. X burttii	Sept. 13	+	
Aug. 22	65	burttii X Koch	Sept. 6		+
Aug. 22	66	Persh. X burttii	Sept. 11	+	
Aug. 22	67	Lotus g. X burttii	Sept. 4		+
Aug. 22	68	Shaw X burttii	Sept. 22	+	
Aug. 22	69	Pring X burttii	Sept. 4	+	
Aug. 23	70	burttii X oval. g.	Sept. 11		+
Aug. 23	71	burttii X Pan. Pac.	Sept. 11		+
Aug. 23	72	Whit. g. X burttii	Sept. 8		+
Aug. 23	73	Pring X burttii	Sept. 8	+	
Aug. 23	74	Persh. X burttii	Sept. 10	+	
Aug. 25	75	burttii X Shaw	Sept. 11		+
Aug. 25	76	Whit. g. X burttii	Sept. 8		+
Aug. 25	77	Persh. X burttii	Sept. 11	+	
Aug. 25	78	Lotus g. X burttii	Sept. 5		+
Aug. 25	79	Hutch. X Sturtev.	Sept. 12	+	
Aug. 26	80	Haarst. X Sturtev.	Sept. 12	+	
Aug. 27	81	burttii X Indep.	Sept. 14	+	

Date of cross	No.	Cross	Date of seed collection	Seed fertile	Seed sterile
Aug. 30	82	burttii X Persh.	Sept. 16		+
Sept. 1	83	burttii X Pring	Sept. 22		+
Sept. 4	84	burttii X Whit. g.	Sept. 22		+
Sept. 7	85	burttii X Stone	Sept. 29		+
Sept. 12	86	burttii X Stella G.	Oct. 2		+
1931					
Aug. 11	87	14 yellow X burttii	Sept. 3	+	
Aug. 11	88	W. Wilson g. X burttii	Sept. 3		+
Aug. 12	89	14 yellow X burttii	Sept. 3	+	
Aug. 12	90	81 dark blue X self	Sept. 3		+
Aug. 12	91	8 yellow X burttii	Sept. 3		+
Aug. 12	92	8 light blue X self	Sept. 3		+
Aug. 12	93	14 yellow X self	Sept. 5	+	
Aug. 12	94	W. Wilson g. X burttii	Sept. 5		+
Aug. 12	95	W. Wilson g. X burttii	Sept. 5		+
Aug. 13	96	81 light blue X self	Sept. 8	+	
Aug. 13	97	8 yellow (wide petals) X burttii	Sept. 3	+	
Aug. 13	98	Persh. X 14	Sept. 3		+
Aug. 14	99	14 yellow X burttii	Sept. 8	+	
Aug. 14	100	7 light blue X self	Sept. 3	+	
Aug. 14	101	W. Wilson g. X burttii	Sept. 8	+	
Aug. 14	102	W. Wilson g. X burttii	Sept. 5	+	
Aug. 16	103	11 light blue X self	Sept. 8		+
Aug. 16	104	81 dark blue X self	Sept. 9	+	
Aug. 15	105	14 yellow X self	Sept. 5		+
Aug. 17	106	13 dark blue X self	Sept. 8	+	
Aug. 17	107	8 yellow X burttii	Sept. 8	+	
Aug. 17	108	Persh. X 14	Sept. 8		+
Aug. 17	109	W. Wilson g. X 7 light blue	Sept. 3	+	
Aug. 18	110	8 yellow (wide petals) X self	Sept. 3		+
Aug. 18	111	8 light blue X self	Sept. 3		+
Aug. 18	112	14 yellow X self	Sept. 8	+	
Aug. 18	113	2 marm. leaf X self	Sept. 3		+
Aug. 18	114	14 yellow X self	Sept. 3	+	
Aug. 18	115	W. Wilson g. X 7 light			

Date of cross	No.	Cross	Date of seed collection	Seed fertile	Seed sterile
		blue	Sept. 8	+	
Aug. 18	116	W. Wilson g. X 7 light blue	Sept. 8	+	
Aug. 18	117	14 yellow X self	Sept. 8		+
Aug. 18	118	11 light blue X self	Sept. 8		+
Aug. 19	119	7 light blue X self	Sept. 12	+	
Aug. 19	120	81 light blue X self	Sept. 12	+	
Aug. 19	121	14 yellow X burttii	Sept. 13	+	
Aug. 19	122	W. Wilson g. X 7 light blue	Sept. 10	+	
Aug. 20	123	13 dark blue X self	Sept. 11	+	
Aug. 20	124	11 light blue X self	Sept. 8		+
Aug. 20	125	8 dark blue X self	Sept. 15	+	
Aug. 20	126	8 yellow (wide petals) X burttii	Sept. 13	+	
Aug. 20	127	14 yellow X self	Sept. 10	+	
Aug. 20	128	W. Wilson g. X 14	Sept. 8	+	
Aug. 20	129	Persh. X 14	Sept. 8	+	
Aug. 21	130	8 light blue X self	Sept. 8		+
Aug. 21	131	14 (copper leaf) X burttii	Sept. 12	+	
Aug. 21	132	13 pink X self	Sept. 14	+	
Aug. 21	133	2 yellow marm. X burttii	Sept. 8	+	
Aug. 21	134	W. Wilson g. X 14	Sept. 8		+
Aug. 22	135	14 yellow X self	Sept. 9	+	
Aug. 22	136	14 yellow X W. Wilson g.	Sept. 12	+	
Aug. 24	137	8 dark blue X self	Sept. 14	+	
Aug. 24	138	burttii X self	Sept. 19	+	
Aug. 24	139	14 yellow (copper leaf) X burttii	Sept. 14	+	
Aug. 24	140	W. Wilson g. X 14	Sept. 15	+	
Aug. 25	141	11 light blue X self	Sept. 12		+
Aug. 25	142	14 yellow (copper leaf) X 14 (green leaf)	Sept. 15	+	
Aug. 25	143	burttii X burttii	Sept. 15	+	
Aug. 25	144	7 light blue X 13 dark blue, vivip.	Sept. 18	+	

Date of cross	No.	Cross	Date of seed collection	Seed fertile	Seed sterile
Aug. 25	145	W. Wil. g. X 13 dark blue, vivip.	Sept. 16	+	
Aug. 25	146	W. Wil. g. X burttii	Sept. 16	+	
Aug. 26	147	13 dark blue X 7 light blue	Sept. 16	+	
Aug. 26	148	W. Wil. g. X 7 light blue	Sept. 17	+	
Aug. 27	149	burttii X 81 dark blue, vivip.	Sept. 12		+
Aug. 27	150	W. Wil. g. X 81 light blue, vivip.	Sept. 13	+	
Aug. 27	151	W. Wil. g. X 81 light blue, vivip.	Sept. 17	+	
Aug. 28	152	burttii X 81 light blue, vivip.	Sept. 22	+	
Aug. 28	153	W. Wil. g. X 81 light blue, vivip.	Sept. 12	+	
Aug. 29	154	13 dark blue, vivip. X burttii	Sept. 18	+	
Aug. 29	155	W. Wil. g. X 13 dark blue, vivip.	Sept. 19	+	
Aug. 29	156	W. Wil. g. X 13 dark blue, vivip.	Sept. 19	+	
Aug. 29	157	81 dark blue X W. Wil. g.	Sept. 14	+	
Aug. 29	158	burttii X W. Wil. g.	Sept. 24	+	
Aug. 31	159	11 dark blue X self	Sept. 13		+
Sept. 8	160	5 light blue X self	Sept. 24	+	
Sept. 14	161	35 light blue X self	Oct. 12	+	
Sept. 15	162	81 cream fl. X self	Oct. 15	+	
Sept. 16	163	7 light blue X self	Oct. 7		+
Sept. 16	164	11 light blue X self	Oct. 2		+
Sept. 17	165	Whit. g. X Pan. White	Oct. 12	+	
Oct. 3	166	35 X self	Oct. 27		+
Oct. 6	167	Eliot X burttii	Oct. 11	+	
1932					
Aug. 16	168	14 X 158 yellow Wilson	Sept. 9	+	
Aug. 9	169	162 yellow, blue-tipped vivip. X self	Sept. 7	+	
Aug. 16	170	162 yellow, blue-tipped			

Nymphaea 'Conqueror'

Nymphaea 'Amabilis'

Nymphaea 'Escarboucle'

Nymphaea 'Sirius'

Nelumbo nucifera

Nymphaea alba

Nymphaea 'Masaniello'

Nymphaea 'Pride of Winterhaven'

Date of cross	No.	Cross	Date of seed collection	Seed fertile	Seed sterile
		vivip. X 158 yellow Wilson	Sept. 11	+	
Aug. 10	171	14 X 107 large yellow	Sept. 10		+
Aug. 9	172	104 violet, vivip. X self	Sept. 7	+	
Aug. 9	173	2 X 158 yellow Wilson	Sept. 13		+
Aug. 16	174	104 violet vivip. X 158 yellow Wilson	Sept. 14	+	
Aug. 10	175	156 type Wilson (more petals) X 104 violet vivip.	Sept. 8	+	
Aug. 10	176	107 dark yellow X 104 pink vivip.	Sept. 8	+	
Aug. 10	177	165 X self	Sept. 3		+
Aug. 9	178	107 good yellow X self	Aug. 29		+
Aug. 10	179	107 dark yellow X 104 pink, vivip.	Sept. 1	+	
Aug. 10	180	99 like burttii X self (dark yellow)	Sept. 10		+
Aug. 11	181	162 yellow vivip. X 158 yellow Wilson (like burttii)	Sept. 3	+	
Aug. 11	182	162 white vivip. X self	Sept. 6	+	
Aug. 11	183	104 pink vivip. X 157 yellow Wilson (like burttii)	Sept. 5	+	
Aug. 11	184	158 light yellow Wilson X 104 violet vivip.	Sept. 9	+	
Aug. 11	185	156 vivip. like Wilson X 104 violet vivip.	Sept. 1	+	
Aug. 11	186	107 dark yellow X 107 dark-yellow special	Aug. 25		+
Aug. 15	187	156 like Wilson X self	Aug. 15		+
Aug. 15	188	158 like burttii X self	Aug. 29		+
Aug. 15	189	104 violet vivip. X 162 yellow vivip.	Sept. 9	+	
Aug. 15	190	104 pink vivip. X 162 yellow vivip.	Sept. 12	+	
Aug. 15	191	2 X 14 St Louis	Aug. 29		+
Aug. 15	192	14 St Louis X 2	Sept. 5	+	

97

Date of cross	No.	Cross	Date of seed collection	Seed fertile	Seed sterile
Aug. 15	193	2 X 107 large dark yellow	Aug. 29		+
Aug. 16	194	107 dark yellow X 158 yellow Wilson	Sept. 3	+	
Aug. 17	195	165 white vivip. X self	Sept. 1		+
Aug. 19	196	132 dark pink X 104 pink vivip.	Sept. 6	+	
Aug. 19	197	Missouri X burttii	Sept. 6		+
Aug. 19	198	2 X 162 yellow vivip.	Sept. 9	+	
Aug. 20	199	156 like Wilson X 156 yellow Wilson	Sept. 11	+	
Aug. 20	200	107 large dark-yellow X 156 yellow Wilson	Sept. 13	+	
Aug. 20	201	104 pink vivip. X 156 yellow Wilson	Sept. 13	+	
Aug. 20	202	107 dark yellow X 162 yellow vivip.	Aug. 31		+
Aug. 20	203	14 St Louis X 162 yellow vivip.	Sept. 13	+	
Aug. 22	204	158 yellow Wilson X self	Aug. 31		+
Aug. 22	205	107 large dark yellow X dark-yellow, like burttii	Sept. 14	+	
Aug. 22	206	99 dark yellow like burttii X self	Sept. 28	+	
Aug. 22	207	burttii X 99 like burttii	Sept. 6	+	
Aug. 22	208	14 X 99 like burttii	Sept. 6	+	
Aug. 23	209	Missouri X self	Sept. 21	+	
Aug. 23	210	158 like burttii X 104 pink vivip.	Sept. 6		+
Aug. 23	211	165 X self (blue)	Sept. 5		+
Aug. 23	212	burttii X self	Sept. 12		+
Aug. 23	213	104 pink vivip. X 144 pink vivip.	Sept. 16	+	
Aug. 23	214	162 yellow vivip. (blue tip) X 107 large yellow	Sept. 17	+	
Aug. 25	215	burttii X self	Sept. 15	+	

Date of cross	No.	Cross	Date of seed collection	Seed fertile	Seed sterile
Aug. 25	216	165 blue X self	Sept. 10		+
Aug. 29	217	light burttii X self	Sept. 24	+	
Aug. 30	218	99 like burttii X self	Sept. 23	+	
Aug. 30	219	162 very light pink X self	Oct. 3	+	
Aug. 30	220	165 blue X self	Sept. 16		+
Aug. 30	221	165 white X self	Sept. 16		+
Aug. 30	222	14 St Louis X 2	Sept. 24	+	
Aug. 30	223	2 X 14 St Louis	Sept. 13		+
Aug. 31	224	158 like burttii X self	Sept. 1		+
Aug. 31	225	156 like Wilson X self	Sept. 19		+
Aug. 31	226	96 salmon-pink X self	Sept 24	+	
Sept. 1	227	Pink Pearl X 162 yellow vivip. (blue tips)	Oct. 3	+	
Sept. 1	228	Edw. C. Eliot X 162 yellow vivip. (blue tips)	Sept. 23	+	
Sept. 1	229	Pan. white X coérulea	Oct. 3	+	
Sept. 2	230	89 yellow cup-shaped X self	Oct. 1		+
Sept. 2	231	122 good blue X self	Oct. 26	+	
Sept. 2	232	Missouri X 162 yellow vivip.	Sept. 19		+
Sept. 2	233	St Louis 14 X 107 large yellow (dark)	Sept. 24		+
Sept. 3	234	106 good blue like Shaw X self	Oct. 17	+	
Sept. 3	235	144 salmon-pink vivip. X self	Oct. 10	+	
Sept. 7	236	152 Indep. yellow X 123 dark red	Oct. 8	+	
Sept. 7	237	135 dark yellow X 123 dark red	Oct. 7	+	
Sept. 8	238	101 cream-coloured X self	Oct. 3		+
Sept. 8	239	158 like burttii X self	Sept. 29		+
Sept. 8	240	96 light blue vivip. X self	Oct. 7	+	
Sept. 13	241	123 red X 152 good			

Date of cross	No.	Cross	Date of seed collection	Seed fertile	Seed sterile
		yellow (blue tips)	Oct. 10	+	
Sept. 14	242	160 good yellow Shaw X self	Oct. 11		+
Sept. 14	243	107 large yellow X Missouri	Oct. 10		+
Sept. 15	244	100 good light pink Koch X self	Nov. 2	+	
Sept. 17	245	87 yellow like burttii X self	Nov. 2	+	
Sept. 17	246	burttii X burttii	Nov. 8	+	
Aug. 17	247	147 white vivip. (pink stamens) X self	Sept. 5		+
Aug. 17	248	123 red X self	Sept. 20	+	
Aug. 19	249	147 white vivip. (pink stamens) X self	Sept. 5		+
Aug. 19	250	151 best Wilson vivip. X self	Sept. 6		+
Aug. 21	251	96 cream vivip. (green leaf) X self	Sept. 8		+
Aug. 21	252	151 best Wilson vivip. X self	Sept. 6		+
Aug. 22	253	104 pink vivip. X self	Sept. 18	+	
Aug. 23	254	123 red X 138 dark yellow	Sept. 12		+
Aug. 23	255	147 white vivip. (pink stamens X 96 rose-pink	Sept. 20	+	
Aug. 23	256	96 rose-pink X self	Sept. 23	+	
Aug. 24	257	151 best Wilson vivip. X self	Sept. 6		+
Aug. 24	258	123 red X 138 dark yellow	Sept. 18	+	
Aug. 25	259	138 dark yellow X self	Sept. 14	+	
Aug. 25	260	151 best Wilson vivip. X 138 dark yellow	Sept. 11	+	
Aug. 26	261	104 pink vivip. X self	Sept. 18	+	
Aug. 26	262	151 best Wilson vivip.			

Date of cross	No.	Cross	Date of seed collec- tion	Seed fertile	Seed sterile
		X 104 pink	Sept. 16	+	
Aug. 26	263	96 white vivip. (green leaf) X self	Sept. 18		+
Aug. 28	264	151 best Wilson vivip. X self	Sept. 11		+
Aug. 28	265	147 white vivip. (pink stamens) X self	Sept. 18	+	
Aug. 29	266	151 best Wilson vivip. X self	Sept. 14		+
Aug. 30	267	96 rose-pink X self	Sept. 26	+	
Aug. 30	268	123 red X self	Sept. 14		+
Aug. 30	269	123 red X 138 dark yellow	Sept. 20		+
Aug. 31	270	138 dark yellow X self	Sept. 18	+	
Aug. 31	271	104 pink vivip. X self	Sept. 25	+	
Sept. 6	272	147 white vivip. (pink stamens) X self	Sept. 29	+	
Sept. 6	273	123 red X self	Sept. 27	+	
Sept. 7	274	246 burttii X self	Oct. 2	+	
Sept. 7	275	151 best Wilson vivip. X self	Sept. 22		+
Sept. 8	276	138 dark yellow X self	Sept. 28	+	
Sept. 8	277	246 burttii X self	Oct. 6	+	
Sept. 8	278	147 white vivip. (pink stamens) X self	Oct. 2	+	
Sept. 13	279	138 dark yellow X 123 red	Oct. 9	+	
Sept. 13	280	96 rose-pink X 138 dark yellow	Oct. 23	+	
Sept. 15	281	246 burttii X self	Oct. 8		+
Sept. 15	282	151 best Wilson vivip. X 246 burttii	Oct. 23	+	
Sept. 15	283	96 white vivip. (green leaf) X 246 burttii	Oct. 23	+	

CHAPTER 10

Garden Pool Construction

The position which a garden pool occupies in relation to other features within the garden is the most important factor influencing the success, or otherwise, of the venture. Apart from the obvious aesthetic considerations, those concerning the welfare of plants and livestock must also be observed if a happy and healthy balance is to be maintained. All aquatic plants, and most especially *Nymphaeas*, enjoy full, uninterrupted sunlight. So do ornamental fish, although they appreciate a cool shady corner in which to glide during the heat of a summer's day. However, it follows that if a pool is placed in full sun abundant plant growth will follow, which in turn will ensure that there is always plenty of surface shade for the fish.

The shape or design of the pool selected is purely a matter of taste, and for the most part has little bearing upon the ultimate success of the plants it contains. However, to be pleasing to the eye it is important that a formal garden should accommodate a formal pool, while an informal or cottage-type garden must have one of irregular design. It is not my intention to dwell upon the rights and wrongs of pool placement within the garden, nor to suggest plant combinations to give various effects. Numerous other publications cover this interesting and very personal aspect of water gardening thoroughly. My main concern here is to ensure that the pool is of sufficient size to accommodate waterlilies and their allies, and is placed in such a position that they may be expected to flourish.

Modern materials have taken much of the hard work out of pool construction. Gone are the days of puddled clay and gault, when the excavation was carefully lined with soot to prevent the earthworms poking holes through the carefully laid finish, and hosepipes were kept at the ready on warm summer days in order to spray the pool walls near ground-level to prevent cracking. However, it would be untruthful to say that building a pool is a simple matter, for much care and hard work is necessary to bring its construction to a successful conclusion; for even with all the modern materials available to the gardener today, the hole has still through necessity to be excavated by hand.

There are a number of different methods of construction to consider. Pool liners are currently the most popular for they are usually comparatively cheap, and will suit any fanciful shape the gardener may care to design. The pool liner consists simply of a sheet of heavy-gauge polythene or rubber material, which is placed in the hole and moulded to the contours of the excavation by the weight of water within, and then secured at the top by rocks or paving slabs.

Selecting a suitable liner often presents the beginner with considerable problems, for he will see that prices vary widely for products which appear to be almost identical.

Those of the lower-price-range are usually of 500-gauge polythene in a sky-blue colour, and made in three or four standard sizes. Obviously mass production of liners like these makes for cheapness, and coupled with the relative ease of present-day polythene manufacture, makes a popular and fast-selling product. However, I would not on the whole recommend the purchase of this kind of liner if any degree of permanency is required. Whilst it is true that with great care a pool of this material will last for upwards of ten years, it is more likely that it will bleach and perish between water-level and ground-level within three or four years, and consequently spring a leak. The most useful purpose to which this kind of liner can be put is as a small hospital pool for sick fish, or temporary accommodation for plants and fish whilst the main pool is being cleaned out.

The pool liners which occupy the medium range are often the best buy for the average gardener as they are durable enough to incorporate as a permanent feature, and yet sufficiently inexpensive as to be within financial reach of the ordinary working man. They are invariably of a polyvinylchloride (PVC) material and available in stone, blue, green or imitation pebble, and whilst many are manufactured to standard sizes, for a few extra pence it is often possible for them to be cut to sizes in accordance with the customer's wishes. Stone and blue are the most popular colours, although manufacturers are producing liners with a stone finish on one side and lagoon blue on the other.

In the more expensive class are the rubber and reinforced PVC liners. The rubber kind are extremely durable and correspondingly expensive. They are invariably of a black matt finish, but can be painted with a specially prepared paint in blue, stone or green. The quality PVC types on the other hand are slightly cheaper than the rubber kind, and differ from their less expensive counterparts by being reinforced with a terylene 'web'. Although visible, this does not detract from its appearance, and makes for a much more durable product.

Having decided upon the type of liner to be employed, it is then necessary to calculate the size. This is done by measuring the length and breadth of the pool or, if it is of an irregular shape, the size of rectangle which will enclose the whole, and then adding on each side the measurement of the deepest part of the pool and the length required to mould into any marginal shelves that are anticipated. A further 9 in (23 cm) or a foot (30 cm) should then be added to each side to allow for anchoring at the top.

Before excavating the hole an idea of the finished shape of the pool can be obtained by taking a length of rope or hosepipe and arranging it in the desired outline, and then placing it in the exact position it will occupy. Thus the surface area and shape can be ascertained accurately. Never start digging with just a vague idea of how the finished pool will appear, for not only may the pool liner turn out to be of the wrong dimensions, but the overall shape of the pool will quite likely not conform with its surroundings. Also, be sure to allow varying depths for different kinds of plants. Deeper areas of a foot (30 cm) to 2½ ft (75 cm) will accommodate various *Nymphaeas* satisfactorily, but most pools benefit from a clump or two of marginal subjects, and these prefer to grow on shallow shelves, 6 or 8 in (15 or 20 cm) deep, and wide enough to take a small container.

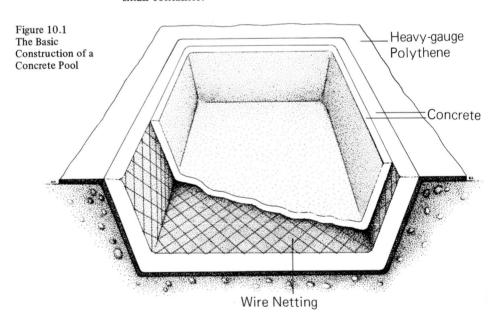

Figure 10.1
The Basic
Construction of a
Concrete Pool

Heavy-gauge Polythene

Concrete

Wire Netting

The digging completed, the hole must be scoured for any sharp objects — stones, sticks, etc. — that are likely to puncture the liner. In gravelly soils or those where flints and similar sharp stones are prevalent, it is advisable to place a thin layer of sand over the floor to act as a cushion, and to line the walls with thick wads of dampened newspaper to prevent any projections from ruining the liner.

Whatever kind of liner is used, the method of installation is more-or-less the same. It is helpful to spread those made from polythene or PVC material out in the sun for an hour or so before working so that they become pliable, and mould to the shape of the excavations more easily.

As a polythene liner has little elasticity it should be installed without water being added, allowing plenty of room for movement so that when introduced it moulds to the exact contours of the hole. PVC and rubber liners can be stretched across the excavation and weighted down with paving slabs or stones. Water is then added, and as the liner tightens, the anchoring weights on the ground are slowly released until the pool becomes full and the liner moulds to its exact shape. When the pool is full, and any unsightly wrinkles that might remain have been dealt with, the surplus material around the sides can be trimmed, allowing just sufficient to remain to enable the liner to be secured by paving slabs or rocks. The pool is then ready for immediate planting, for none of the specially designed pool liners contain any harmful elements likely to prove toxic to aquatic life.

This latter quality is also responsible in no small measure for the increased popularity of pre-shaped pools of plastic or fibre-glass, for although the cost of these and concrete ones are comparable, one does not have the tedious task of scrubbing or soaking the surface in order to get rid of the effects of free lime before planting can begin. The cheaper brands of this kind of pool are usually vacuum moulded in a tough, weather-resistant plastic, and have a roughish, undulating finish to simulate natural rock. Whilst being inexpensive and easily transportable, they do have the disadvantage of flexibility, which can cause difficulty during installation, whereas those made from fibre-glass are entirely rigid and free-standing. However, they are comparatively inexpensive, and many beginners are tempted to try the plastic variety before investing in a more permanent job.

But for the experienced pond owner and the confident or affluent novice, a fibre-glass pool is a splendid investment. It is virtually indestructible, and if treated with respect will last a lifetime. There are dozens of different shapes and sizes, most of which can be obtained in a stone, blue, white or green colouring, and I would suggest that a prospective customer sends for several of the excellent illustrated and informative catalogues currently being issued by manufacturers, before making a final choice.

But a word of warning: pools that are described as 'rock pools' or 'fountain trays' are not suitable for plants or fish, and although many gardeners are attracted by their comparative cheapness, they should read the manufacturers' descriptions carefully before

Figure 10.2
Pool Construction
in Detail Using
a Pool Liner

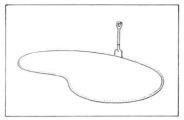

Lay out a rope or hose to the required shape and size of the pool adjusting until all aspects are satisfactory. Cut out the outline of the pool and dispense with the rope. Always cut inside to allow for final trimming.

Cut the sides with an inward slope 3" (8 cm) in for every 9" (23 cm) down. A marginal shelf should be incorporated as required.

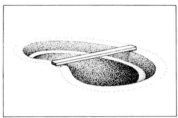

Using a spirit level check the top of the pool is level. Check that the depth of the marginal shelf is correct.

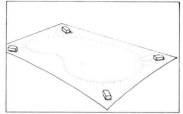

Remove any sharp protrusions and lay sand on base and dampened newspaper around sides. Drape the liner loosely into the excavation with an even overlap. Place weights on the liner.

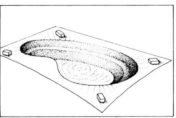

As the pool fills the weights should be eased off at intervals to allow the liner to fit snugly into the excavation.

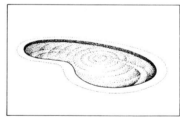

When the pool is filled waste material should be trimmed off with scissors leaving a 4" (10 cm) overlap.

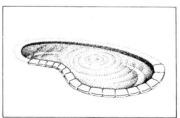

The paving should be laid on a mortar mix of 3 parts sand/1 part cement with an overhang of 2" (5 cm) over the pool.

The finished pool after planting. Rockeries, fountains and waterfalls can be added after completion of the pool.

106

purchasing. 'Rock pools' are those designed to sit near the summit of a rock garden and from which water tumbles down a cascade unit into a lower pool. They hold a very small volume of water and cannot sustain any aquatic life, save possibly that of a handful of water snails and a couple of oxygenating plants. 'Fountain trays' are also too shallow; these are the type of pool in which a fountain alone is stood or into which a gargoyle may spout. Owing to the turbulence of water created in this environment little of any significance can be grown, and although ornamental fish would survive they would not be very happy.

Installing a pre-shaped pool is not terribly difficult if one knows how to tackle the job properly. Unfortunately, most people attempt to dig out a hole in the shape of the pool — a method doomed to failure. A more practical approach is to dig out a rectangle to enclose the entire outline of the pool. Then place the pool on a thin layer of sand and, by means of bricks and similar materials, level it up so that from side to side and end to end it is completely level and approximately an inch below the surface of the surrounding ground. The levelling ensures that when the pool is filled, the water lies evenly and does not drain to one corner and over onto the lawn. The idea of the pool being lower than ground level is so that when back-filling takes place the lifting of the pool, which is inevitable when soil is rammed evenly around it, is no more than can be comfortably camouflaged when the job is finished. In soils that are stony or heavy and in poor tilth it is better to back-fill with sand, gradually removing any supporting bricks as the filling replaces them. This should be rammed tightly around the pool, as any air pockets behind it may give rise to subsidence in years to come.

Finally, we come to concrete, which if laid properly is still the best form of construction. Not only can it be prepared in several colours, but can be formed into almost any shape imaginable. The excavation should be taken out 6 in (15 cm) larger than the desired finished size, the soil firmed, and then lined with polythene or building paper before operations commence. It is best if the concreting can be done in one day as there is then less likelihood of a leak occurring. If this proves to be impossible, then the edges of the first day's concreting should be 'roughed up' so that the next day's concrete mixes with it. No more than twenty-four hours should elapse between joining any one batch of concrete and another if the possibility of leaking is to be avoided.

Although mixing concrete is hard physical work, there is nothing complicated or mysterious about it. A good mixture consists of one part cement, two parts sand and four parts ¾-in (20 mm) gravel measured out with a shovel or bucket. This is then mixed in its dry state until of a uniform greyish colour. If a waterproofing compound

107

is to be added, it should be done at this stage.

Proprietary brands such as 'Medusa' and 'Pudlo' come in a powder form, and should be mixed in with the aggregate strictly according to the manufacturers' instructions. Water is then added and mixing continued until the agglomeration is of a wet, yet stiff, nature. A good guide to its readiness is to place a shovel into the mixture and withdraw it in a series of jerks; if the ridges thus formed retain their formation, the concrete is ready for laying.

It should be spread evenly to a depth of 4 in (10 cm) over the floor and, if the slope of the sides permits, up these as well. Wire netting can then be placed on the concrete and trapped between the base and final layers to act as reinforcement. The final layer of 2 in (5 cm) is then laid, and given a smooth finish with a plasterer's trowel. If the pool sides are vertical or very steep, formwork may have to be erected. This is usually of rough timber and held in place to form a mould for the walls. To reduce the risk of the concrete sticking to the timbers, they should, strictly speaking, be greased or limewashed, but one can usually get away with soaking the boards in water before pouring the concrete behind them.

When the pool is to be of an irregular shape and the harsh straightness of ordinary planks is undesirable, a successful result can usually be achieved by the careful use of plywood or other pliable material — suitably strengthened with ordinary timbers — and bent to the various contours that are desired.

When a coloured finish is required, the necessary ingredients should be added at the dry-mix stage of the concrete used for the final layer. Pigments mixed in with the cement in any proportion up to 10 per cent by weight of the same, give a good, even colouring. Red iron oxide provides a red colouring, chromium oxide a deep green, cobalt blue a blue, and manganese black a black; whilst the use of Snowcrete cement and fine Derbyshire spar produces a really first-class, white finish.

A couple of hours after completion, when any lingering surface water from the concrete has soaked away, all the exposed areas of concrete should be covered with wet sacks, especially if the weather is warm and sunny. This prevents the concrete from drying too rapidly and hair-cracks appearing. If the area to be covered is large, then regular spraying of the surface with water from a watering can with a fine rose attachment is to be recommended. Depending upon the weather, but after about five days, the concrete should have 'gone off', and be ready for treating prior to the introduction of plants and livestock.

As is well known, concrete contains a substantial amount of free lime, which can be harmful in varying degrees to both plant and fish life. Leaving the pool to the mercy of the elements for about six months is the easiest method of preventing trouble occurring, but few gardeners are prepared to wait this long before introducing some kind of life. Many treatments are recommended by different authorities, and include scrubbing the concrete with potassium permanganate, emptying and refilling the pool upwards of half a dozen times and many other laborious and dubious methods. From personal experience, I would suggest filling the pool with water once and leaving it to stand for a week or ten days and then emptying. When the concrete has dried, an application of a neutralising agent, such as the well-known 'Silglaze' compound, should completely eliminate the chance of any trouble occurring.

It is also perhaps worth mentioning that in neutralising the lime, a product of this nature reacts to form silica — an insoluble compound — and thus seals the concrete by internal glazing. Rubber-based and liquid plastic paints, when painted over the entire concrete surface, also prevent free lime from escaping but in most cases it must be remembered that a special primer has to be applied first to prevent a chemical reaction between concrete and paint. These paints are available in several pleasing pastel shades and give a splendid finish to the pool, but unfortunately prove rather expensive when there are large areas to be covered.

CHAPTER 11

Hardy Waterlily Culture

There are two techniques commonly advocated for the culture of hardy *Nymphaeas* and *Nuphars*. Either the pool floor can be covered with 6 in (15 cm) or so of prepared compost and the plants grown directly in this, or else they can be planted in some kind of container, a box or basket. Most gardeners prefer to adopt the latter method, for then the plants can be easily removed for inspection or division, or in the event of the pool needing to be cleaned out. Specially manufactured waterlily baskets are the best, and are readily available from most horticultural sundriesmen. Usually they are of a heavy-gauge, rigid polythene or plastic material and of a design that will not easily become unbalanced and topple over in the water. Occasionally an old-fashioned lily basket or wooden planting crate may be encountered, and these will be just as suitable although not quite so durable. As both baskets and crates have lattice-work sides, it is advisable to line them with hessian before planting (Figures 11.1-11.3).

Contrary to popular belief, there is nothing mysterious about the compost used for planting waterlilies. Good, clean garden soil from land that has not recently been dressed with artificial fertiliser is the main constituent. It should be thoroughly sieved, and care taken to remove twigs, pieces of turf, weeds, old leaves or indeed anything likely to decompose and foul the water. On no account should soil be collected from wet, low-lying land or natural ponds or streams, as this will often contain the seeds of pernicious water weeds which may be difficult to eradicate at a later date.

The soil having been prepared, a little coarse bonemeal should be added. Allow about a handful for each basket to be planted, and mix it thoroughly into the compost. A coarse grade of hoof and horn or similar slow-acting nitrogenous fertiliser may also be used, but only sparingly, and not in the popular powdered or granular form, as this will usually cloud the water and may even prove toxic to the fish. Old gardening books often recommend the liberal use of rotted farmyard manure or cow dung in waterlily composts. However, I have found this to be undesirable, for unless great care is taken to

Figure 11.1
Cutting a Square of
Hessian for a
Planting Basket

Figure 11.2
Lining the Basket
with Hessian

Figure 11.3
Partially Filled
Basket with Surplus
Hessian Removed

ensure that it does not come into direct contact with the water, pollution is likely to occur.

Waterlilies can be planted in Great Britain at any time from late April until mid-August. The compost used should be made to such a consistency that when squeezed in the hand it binds together, yet is not so wet as to allow water to ooze out through the fingers. Before planting have a close look at the rootstocks of the waterlilies involved. Those of *Nymphaea odorata* and *N. tuberosa* varieties have long, white fleshy rhizomes, and should be set horizontally about an inch (25 mm) beneath the surface of the compost with just the crown exposed. The Marliacea and Laydekeri hybrids, together with many intermediate varieties and the *Nuphars*, have bulky, log-like rootstocks with fibrous roots arranged like a ruff, immediately beneath the crown. These are planted vertically, or at a slight angle, with the crown just protruding above the planting medium.

Figure 11.4
Preparing the
Waterlily for
Planting —
Removing Dead
Tissue, etc.

It is advisable before planting to remove all the adult leaves at the point where they emerge from the crown (Figure 11.4). This may seem drastic, but they would in all probability die anyway, and when planted with the foliage intact this often acts as a float, giving the plant buoyancy and lifting it right out of the basket. Similarly, the fibrous roots should be cut back to the rootstock, and any dead or decaying area of the rhizome pared back with a knife to live tissue and dressed with powdered charcoal to help seal the wound. If a rootstock takes on a gelatinous appearance and is evil-smelling, avoid allowing it to make contact with other sound varieties, for this is a certain indication of infection with the waterlily root-rot.

When planting, be sure that the compost is packed as tightly as possible in the container, for it will be full of air spaces, and will decrease considerably in volume as the water drives the air out

112

Figure 11.5
Planting the
Waterlily in a Heavy
Loam Compost

Figure 11.6
Filling the Basket to
Within an Inch or so
of the Top

Figure 11.7
Covering the Basket
with a Layer of Pea
Shingle

(Figures 11.5, 11.6). Rootstocks of newly planted waterlilies may be left completely exposed following this sinking effect, and in many cases where their roots have not had a chance to penetrate the compost the whole plant will come floating to the surface. Watering newly planted waterlilies like pot plants prior to placing in their permanent quarters, usually helps to settle the compost and alleviates much of this trouble. A layer of washed pea shingle about an inch (25 mm) deep should be spread over the surface of the planting medium to discourage fish from nosing in the compost and clouding the water (Figure 11.7). However, this should not be collected from the seashore, as it will have a high salt content which may prove detrimental to the other inhabitants of the pool.

Place the planted baskets in position in the pool and run in enough water to cover their crowns. Then, as the young foliage appears, gradually raise the level of the water. Never plunge the waterlilies directly into 2 or 3 ft (60-90 cm) of cold water unless absolutely necessary, for they have already suffered a considerable shock by being moved and defoliated whilst in active growth. When merely adding to your collection, or replacing a dead or overgrown waterlily in an existing pond, then this procedure can be reversed. The basket is stood on a pile of bricks and lowered gradually one by one as the growths lengthen. When baskets have to be placed in an awkward position in the centre of a pool, lengths of string can be threaded through either side of the basket, and with one person each side of the pool can be carefully lowered into place (Figure 11.8).

Figure 11.8
Lowering a Basket
into the Deep End

When planting into compost on the pool floor all the same general rules apply. It follows though, that if a hosepipe is placed directly into the pool and turned on, the water will stir up the soil and become cloudy, but by placing the end of the hosepipe on a

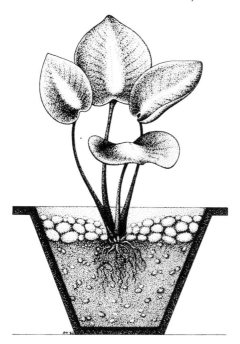

Figure 11.9
A Waterlily is
Planted in Soil with
a Layer of Gravel
Above

Figure 11.10
Submerged
Oxygenating Plants
are Planted with
Buried Lead Weights

Lead Weight

large sheet of polythene and allowing the water to trickle over the edges this is prevented. As the water level rises the polythene is lifted and trapped against the end of the hosepipe, which if the sheet is large enough, will also be gradually raised until the water is at the desired level.

Gardeners who are fortunate enough to have natural ponds have to adopt a different planting technique. This often conflicts with established practice and is usually only effective because stronger and more vigorous varieties are used in such situations. As it is impractical to empty such a pond, plants have to be planted through the water. The best method is to plant them in prepared compost on squares of hessian, the four corners of which are then lifted and tied just beneath the crown. These 'packages' can then be gently placed in the water and allowed to sink to the bottom. The hessian will eventually rot, by which time the plants will be well established in the compost and probably have penetrated the surrounding mud on the pool floor. In large expanses of water where groups of waterlilies are required, they can be planted two or three together in a wooden orange box, taken out in a boat and gently lowered over the side.

The positioning of waterlilies in the pool is dependent upon a number of factors. First is the depth of water available, which in turn determines, within limits, the varieties which can be safely grown in a given situation. The presence of moving water reduces the number of plants which can be accommodated, for few varieties will tolerate even the slightest movement in the water, and are therefore totally unsuitable for streams, or pools where a fountain is constantly playing. Sunlight is another important consideration, and plants should be placed in positions where they will receive the maximum amount. Where none, or only a few of these necessary conditions exist, then it is advisable to look at the possibilities of substituting with varieties of *Nuphar*, for they are more tolerant of the conditions which the *Nymphaeas* abhor.

Although a waterlily pool is initially a time-consuming feature of the garden, once established its maintenance is relatively simple and undemanding. Routine care consists of keeping an eye open for pests and diseases, lifting and dividing the plants every third or fourth year and regular feeding, for both *Nymphaeas* and *Nuphars*, in common with many terrestial plants, are gross feeders.

Unfortunately, difficulty is often experienced in getting fertiliser down to the roots without lifting and replanting in fresh compost or considerably fouling the water. A certain degree of success can be achieved, however, by making 'bonemeal pills', which are dropped in the water alongside the plants. These are made with a handful of coarse bonemeal with sufficient wet clay to bind it together. Where plants are growing in baskets, these 'pills' can be pushed into the soil

Figure 11.12
A Well-planted Pool

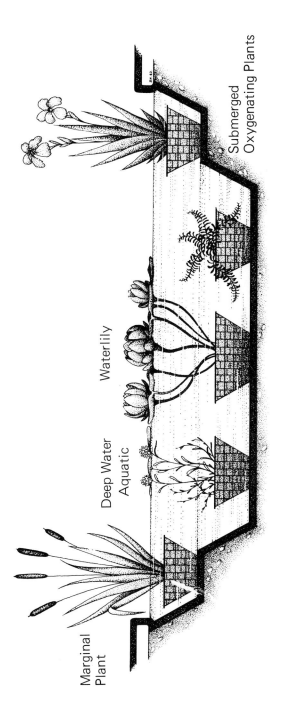

Submerged
Oxygenating Plants

Waterlily

Deep Water
Aquatic

Marginal
Plant

117

next to the roots. The frequency with which this operation should be carried out will vary greatly according to the variety and compost, but its need will be apparent when the leaves of the plant become yellowish and get progressively smaller and the blooms are of poor colour, with fewer petals, and are more or less abortive.

Apart from feeding the waterlilies, the only other major factor to contend with is algae control. Aquatic algae occur in various forms, but notably free-floating and filamentous. The free-floating or yellow-green algae consist of some four hundred different species which live mainly in fresh water or occasionally on mud. They are generally about the size of a pin head, and occur in their millions to create a green 'bloom' or pea soup effect. The filamentous algae on the other hand appear as free-floating spirogyra, which can be dragged from the pond by the handful, or else in thick mats known as blanket or flannel weed. Other kinds, like the so-called 'mermaid's hair', cling to plants and baskets, often coating the walls of the pond as well.

Control of the free-floating kinds is relatively easy with an algaecide based on potassium permanganate, but it must be treated on a dull day when the water is not too warm, otherwise the pool with turn a thick, cloudy yellow and have to be emptied. Filamentous algae can be controlled with proprietary algaecides like Algymicin PLL, but after treatment all dead algae must be removed to prevent deoxygenation of the water.

Gardeners with a more scientific turn of mind can control algae much more economically and just as successfully with straight chemicals. Indeed, in large expanses of water this is the only practical way of doing so. Copper sulphate is undoubtedly the best, for in small regular doses it can be safely used when fish are present. Where fish are not present it can be used at a greater strength, being harmless to all higher plants while controlling the algae quickly and effectively. It might also be mentioned that under these conditions the stronger copper sulphate application is usually sufficient to control aquatic pests like caddis fly, and will curtail waterlily root-rot and fungal leaf-spots too.

For successful algae control where fish are present a concentration of 0.33 ppm introduced on alternate days over the period of a fortnight usually clears all algal growth. Treated in this manner the water seldom suffers oxygen depletion, and the fish are not subjected to asphyxiation by the copper sulphate combining with their body mucus, as is often the case with higher concentrations.

In very hard water this dosage may need to be slightly increased, as copper sulphate unites with the carbonate of the calcium carbonate to form an insoluble precipitate of copper carbonate. It is therefore essential to test the pH of the water. The water temperature at the time of the application should also be ascertained, as this may have an affect upon the reaction; for it is likely that the unstable calcium bicarbonate normally found in tap water would leave a higher concentration of calcium carbonate in warmer weather, thereby reducing the effect of the copper sulphate. However, if there are no fish present in the pond, a dosage of 2 ppm will kill all the algae at one go.

Formalin is sometimes used in the control of algae, but a great deal more needs to be known about its effect on various plants before its use can be given an unqualified recommendation. A solution of 1 part to 4,000 destroys free-floating algae and is said to be beneficial to cyprinid fish, but it induces several cultivars of *Nymphaea* into rapid growth, with leaf stalks becoming extended by 2 or 3 ft (60-90 cm), and in the case of the deep-water aquatic *Nymphoides peltata*, destroys it completely.

No form of algae control is permanent, but the most stable is embraced by the theory of natural balance, in which submerged oxygenating plants compete with the more primitive algae for the dissolved mineral salts in the water. If planted in sufficient quantities they starve the algae out of existence, and in conjunction with the foliage of waterlilies and floating aquatics, which reduce the amount of sunlight falling directly into the water, they create a healthy, clear, well-oxygenated pool. The chemical controls described earlier merely prevent algae gaining a hold in the pool until the plants have become established.

Feeding the plants and algae control are primarily tasks for the spring and summer months; however, the pool is not as lifeless as it may seem during the autumn and winter, and a number of routine tasks must be performed. The first essential is to clean up the marginal plants immediately the first autumn frosts have turned the foliage brown, removing any dead or decaying material likely to pollute the water or harbour over-wintering insect pests.

The waterlilies themselves can be allowed to die down naturally, but any yellow leaves with soft, crumbling edges or black, spreading blotches should be regarded with suspicion and immediately removed, as this could well be a sign of a waterlily leaf-spot. Many gardeners feel concern for their waterlilies during winter, but they need not fear, for as long as there is between 9 in (23 cm) and a foot (30 cm) of water covering the crowns they will be perfectly alright. Small and pygmy varieties that may be growing in a shallow rock pool can have the water drained off and the crowns covered with a generous layer of old leaves or straw for winter protection. When the fear of sharp frosts has abated, they can easily be restarted into growth by the addition of water.

Although the propagation of waterlilies may never occur to the gardener with a couple of plants in his pool, it is, nevertheless, an interesting facet of waterlily culture which should not be neglected. It will probably come as a surprise to many to learn that only two kinds of hardy waterlily, *N. tetragona* and *N. pygmaea* 'Alba' are commonly grown from seed in this country. Most hardy hybrids grown today are infertile, and even those that do set viable seed take so long to come to maturity and will probably not be true to type when grown this way, that it is not a method usually worthwhile contemplating.

The seeds of both *N. tetragona* and *N. pygmaea* 'Alba' form in greenish-white fruits which become submerged immediately the flowers fade. They re-appear at the surface again some three weeks later, and if not collected immediately will burst open and scatter their contents into the water. The pods should be gathered after they have been submerged for about ten days, detached with as much old flower stem as possible, and placed in a shallow dish of water so that when they ripen the seed will not be lost. Alternatively, a small muslin bag can be used to enclose the seed pod and removed from the plant immediately the pod dehisces. When the fruits are ripe they will be clearly seen to exude a clear, gelatinous substance in which the seeds are embodied. No attempt should be made to separate them from this protective coating, but the whole sticky mass sown intact.

Finely sieved, clean garden soil without the addition of fertiliser is the best sowing medium, and should be put in shallow seed pans. The seeds are then sown in as near a manner as possible to that advocated for most terrestial plants, the jelly being spread evenly over the surface of the compost with a pair of tweezers. A light covering of soil is given and the pans sprayed gently overhead from a watering can in order to settle the compost. They can then be stood in a bowl or aquarium with the water just lapping over the surface of the compost, and placed in a warm, sunny position.

After three weeks or so the first seedlings will appear. They have tiny, translucent, more-or-less lanceolate leaves, and look like an aquatic form of liverwort. During this time, and indeed for the first six months of their lives, filamentous algae are likely to cause trouble by becoming entwined amongst the fragile, juvenile foliage. This can usually be controlled quite simply by the prompt use of a proprietary algaecide. However, it is essential to remove the destroyed remains of the algae or else fermentation will occur with subsequent rotting of the *Nymphaea* foliage. When the first two or three small, floating leaves have come to the surface the plants can be pricked out. They should be lifted in clumps, washed thoroughly to remove all the soil, and then gently teased apart. A standard plastic seed tray or plastic half pots are the most useful containers in which to prick out the seedlings, which should then be immersed so that the compost is about an inch (25 mm) beneath the surface of the water. This level, however, can be raised considerably as the growths lengthen and become much stronger. After six or seven months the plants will begin to crowd one another, at which time they should be lifted and moved to their permanent quarters.

Apart from the two varieties just mentioned, all other varieties of hardy *Nymphaea* and to a lesser degree the *Nuphars*, can be propagated by 'eyes' and indeed in most cases this is common commercial practice. 'Eyes' are tiny growing points which occur with varying frequency along the rootstocks of mature, hardy waterlilies. In most cases they appear as smaller versions of the main growing point, each with its own juvenile foliage seeming ready to burst into active growth, although in *Nymphaea tuberosa* and its varieties they take the form of brittle, rounded nodules which are easily detached.

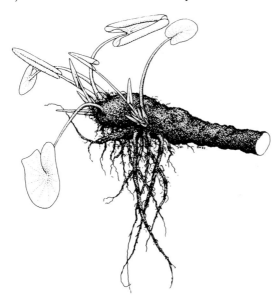

Figure 11.13
A Typical Hybrid
Hardy Waterlily
Ready for Planting.
The 'eye' can be
quite clearly seen

Parent plants should be lifted during April or May and the 'eyes' removed with a sharp knife. The wounds of both 'eye' and rootstock are dusted with powdered charcoal to prevent infection and the rootstock returned to the pool. The 'eyes' are then potted individually in small pots in a good, stiff, loam compost, and stood in a shallow container to which has been added sufficient water to cover the rims of the pots. If the 'eyes' are very small it is advisable to give them the added protection of a cold frame or greenhouse during the early stages of growth. As they grow the water level must be raised, and the plants potted in successively larger pots until a 4-in (10 cm) size is attained, after which it can be safely assumed that they will be

121

capable of holding their own in the outdoor pool.

Whether or not it is thought desirable that the plants be propagated, there comes a time when an established clump must be divided. This is indicated by a preponderance of leafy growth in the centre of the plant, which thrusts upwards and above the surface of the water, often accompanied by diminishing flower size. With most kinds this condition manifests itself after the plant has remained undisturbed for three or four years, although some of the smaller growing varieties may go for as long as six or seven years without needing attention. May is the best time to divide waterlilies in Great Britain, each plant being lifted and washed, and any adult foliage removed at source.

It will be seen that each plant consists of a main rootstock from which several 'eyes' have grown to form sizeable 'branches', and it is these side growths that should be retained, cutting them from the parent plant with as much healthy young rootstock as possible. The thick, bulky part of the original plant is generally of little use and should be discarded, but all the 'branches' can be planted individually to form new plants, providing of course that they each have a healthy terminal shoot.

CHAPTER 12

Tropical Waterlily Culture

There are a number of different methods of growing tropical water-lilies, but in Great Britain they are usually confined to tubs or a heated pool, although with a little attention they will flourish as temporary inhabitants of the outdoor pool. Even in warmer climates, although they will over-winter outside, they are best treated as temporary subjects and replanted each spring, and the suggestions for their culture which follow, apply.

Upon arrival from the nurseries in early spring, the plants are in a dormant state and appear as rather coarse, rounded, chestnut-like tubers. They should be inspected immediately for soft areas on the surface, and when soaked in water for an hour or so should become heavy and sink; those that do not are likely to be of little use, remaining dormant for several months, or just rotting away and leaving an empty, scaly skin behind.

Once satisfied that the tubers are absolutely sound, pot them individually in 3-in (8 cm) pots in the same compost as recommended for their hardy counterparts (see page 110). Stand the pots in an aquarium or shallow tray of water, in a temperature of between 65° and 70°F (18° and 21°C) and place in a position of full sunlight. After a few days juvenile underwater foliage will appear, followed a week or so later by the rounded, floating, adult leaves. At this stage the plants can be transferred to their permanent quarters. If one or two tubers have shown no signs of sprouting by this time, remove them from their pots, repot in coarse, washed sand and return them to the tray or aquarium. For some inexplicable reason this is often enough to jog them into active growth, after which they can be potted once again in ordinary compost.

When tubs are used for planting, these often prove to be second-hand barrels which have been sawn in half and made water-tight. Whilst not wishing to condemn a gardener's enterprise, I do think that a few words are in order at this point regarding the suitability of barrels that have previously contained substances other than water. Old wine or vinegar casks are admirable, as are beer barrels, but those which have contained fats, oils, tar or wood preservative

123

should be avoided, as any residue that remains will pollute the water, forming an unsightly scum on the surface. Before attempting to plant anything in a newly made tub, give it a good scrubbing inside with clear water, and then thoroughly rinse it out. On no account use detergent for cleaning, as it is difficult to be sure when all traces have been removed. Tubs that have been used before often become coated on the inside with a thick growth of slime and algae, and where it is felt that water alone is an insufficient cleaning agent, then the addition of enough potassium permanganate to turn the water a violet colour will usually have the desired effect.

By the time the waterlilies are ready to plant in their permanent home, it is late spring or early summer. They should be planted with their crowns just protruding above the soil, only one plant being allowed to each tub, and even then some of the larger varieties will be cramped. Water is added gradually as the plant grows and should be kept at a temperature of between 55° and 60°F (12° and 15°C). The advantage with tub culture is that this can easily be done by the introduction of an ordinary aquarium heater, which rapidly warms up small bodies of water and, in conjunction with a thermostat to control the temperature, proves to be a particularly cheap and efficient means of heating.

Planting in the pool is almost identical, except that the plants should remain potted for a greater length of time, being moved to successively larger pots until in full growth. The main reason for doing this is to give them a good start when plunged into deep water, for small, sprouted tubers often have a tremendous struggle to become established under such conditions, whereas a large plant removed from its pot with rootball intact, will hardly realise it has been transplanted and will grow away vigorously.

Nothing much need be done with the plants during the summer months, except for the periodic check for pests, and when the plants are grown in tubs, ensuring that these are topped up regularly. When autumn approaches and the nights start drawing in, the water should be gradually lowered and the mud allowed to dry out, or in the garden pool the baskets removed and dried out slowly. This causes the top growth to die away and ripens the tubers, which are then lifted for storing. Damp sand is the best medium to store them in, and should be contained in a vermin-proof box of some kind and kept in a frost-proof place. I use an old cake tin, in which I lay the tubers out in rows sandwiched between inch-deep (25 mm) layers of sand. They keep very well for the winter months without any attention, and should not be interfered with until planting time the following spring. Many growers do not even bother with storing, but treat the plants as annuals and purchase fresh stock each year. Indeed, this has much to commend it, for young tubers are often more active and grow into far superior plants than the older, woody ones.

Unlike their hardy counterparts, most tropical *Nymphaea* species can be grown successfully from seed, the procedure to be adopted differing little from that advocated earlier. The seeds are sown in pans of sandy compost and placed in water that is maintained at a steady temperature of 75°-80°F (23°-27°C). Once the first floating leaves have developed, the plants may be potted and kept at the same temperature in full sunlight for the winter months. I find that it is imperative to keep them actively growing during the first winter, or they will almost certainly rot whilst lying dormant in the damp compost. Collection of the tubers in the autumn is out of the question, for they are so minute as to need a hand lens to be able to see them.

Conversely, though surprisingly, it is almost impossible to over-winter the large tubers which many varieties of tropical waterlilies seem to make, but most of them will in fact form a tiny tuber, about the size of a chestnut, at the base of the main crown which can be successfully stored. Nocturnal varieties and hybrids derived from *N. colorata* bear masses of spawn, or small tubers, on the surface of the parent as well as beneath, and should receive similar treatment.

In the early spring the young tubers can be potted about 2 in (5 cm) deep in a sandy compost, and the pots stood in water at a steady temperature of 70°F (21°C) in a sunny position. After about two weeks the young leaves will start to appear. When the first true, floating leaves have developed, locate with thumb and forefinger the stem-like growth connecting the young plant to the tuber. Follow this growth down and carefully pinch it off just above the tuber, removing the young plant with its root intact, but leaving the tuber in its pot. The young plant should be immediately potted and placed in a heated aquarium with a temperature of 70°-75°F (21°-23°C). In two or three weeks the original propagating tuber will send up another plant, which can also be removed and potted. This may be repeated for three or four times before the tuber is allowed to retain the final plant.

The viviparous or live-bearing group of tropical waterlilies are the ones which bear young plants in the leaf sinus. The frequency of occurrence and strength of growth of these young plants varies greatly with locality, those varieties reproducing viviparously in warm climates often not doing so in cooler areas. But as light and day length are believed to be major contributing factors in these differences, the gardener can do much to assist proliferation in tub-grown plants by giving several hours of extended daylight with an ordinary tungsten-filament lamp.

As young plants on the leaves develop roots, they should be

removed and potted individually in small pots of sandy compost, and then stood in water which is maintained at a temperature of 60°-65°F (15°-18°C), potting them into progressively larger pots as the need arises. They will probably grow strongly throughout the first winter, and may even flower, but one need not feel any concern, for this is merely a sign of well-being.

One drawback to this method of propagation, however, is the preponderance of multi-headed plants which occur. They will generally have smaller flowers than the single-headed forms raised from tubers, and produce irregularly placed clumps of leaves on the surface of the water. Not much can be done to alleviate this condition once a plant has become well established, but practically all viviparous waterlilies can be readily divided into single plants whilst in the formative period.

The young plants must be removed from their pots as soon as the clusters of terminal growths are discernible, and a knife used to cut sharply through the thickening tissues where the new tubers are forming. By doing this, several tiny plants with roots attached can be removed from each individual tuber, and then potted up and grown on in the usual manner.

CHAPTER 13

Nuphars

The *Nuphars* or spatterdocks are usually regarded as poor relations of the *Nymphaeas*. But what they lack in the way of flowers, they more than amply compensate for with their ease of cultivation and adaptability to situation. They will thrive in dense shade or full sun, flowing streams or stagnant ponds, and there are species to suit all depths of water from a few inches (cm) up to 8 ft (2 m 50 cm). Most have beautiful membraneous, translucent, submerged foliage, and some of the smaller kinds are used by aquarists as centre-pieces in cold-water aquaria. Cultivation is identical to that afforded to the various *Nymphaea* species, and propagation is usually by division, although 'eyes' are sometimes produced.

Nuphar advena American Spatterdock, Mooseroot. This is a popular, fairly common, but very variable species which will grow either in sun or shade. Some of the large, thick, fresh-green leaves float on the surface of the water, while others stand erect from the vigorous crown. The globular yellow flowers are about 3 in (18 cm) across, are tinged with purple or green, and have bright coppery-red stamens. N. America. (1½-5 ft (45 cm-1 m 50 cm)).

N. advena var. *brevifolia* This plant has much smaller leaves with petioles oval in cross-section, and the flowers are about half the diameter and rarely tinged with purple. N. America. (1½-4 ft (45 cm-1 m 20 cm)).

N. advena var. *macrophylla* Very little is known of this plant except that it has a reputation for being happy in fast-flowing water, and most botanists regard it as a geographical form of the species. It has a restricted distribution through Florida and the southern United States. (1½-4 ft (45 cm-1 m 20 cm)).

N. advena var. *orbiculata*, *N. orbiculata* This is a vigorous plant with bright-green, rounded and pubescent leaves with fluted edges. The pale-yellow blossoms are about 2 in (5 cm) in diameter. S. United States. (1-3 ft (30-90 cm)).

N. advena var. *variegata* See *N. variegata*.

Species and their Varieties

127

Figure 13.1 *Nuphar advena* showing Plant with Thick Rootstock x ¼ (a), Flower x ½ (b), Fruit x ½ (c), Cross-section of Fruit x 1 (d), a Bay-like Section from a Fruit containing Several Seeds x 1 (e) and Seed x 3 (f); *N. variegatum* showing Seed x 3 (g) and Leaf x ½ (h)

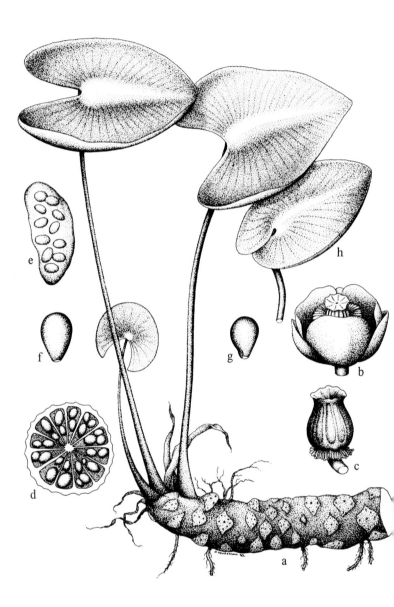

N. americana See *N. variegata*.

N. americanum See *N. advena*.

N. fraterna The small, sharply pointed leaves are rarely more than 6 in (15 cm) long, with strangely flattened petioles; and the tiny, yellow flowers are no more than an inch (25 mm) across. New Jersey. (1½-3 ft (45-90 cm)).

N. japonica Japanese Pond Lily. This has large, slender, arrow-shaped floating leaves and curled, translucent, underwater foliage. The small yellow flowers are up to 3 in (8 cm) across. It does well only in still water. The natural distribution is restricted to the islands of Kyushu, Shikoku, Hokkaide and Honshu, Japan. (1-2½ ft (45-75 cm)).

N. japonica var. *rubrotincta* The glowing-orange flowers with their red-tipped stamens are held above fine, upstanding, brownish or olive-green foliage. It is known only from cultivation. (1½-2½ ft (45-75 cm)).

N. japonica var. *rubrotincta gigantea* This is a dull orange-flowered form which is larger in all its parts. (1-3 ft (30-90 cm)).

N. japonica var. *variegata* The foliage is mottled with cream and green, and the small flowers are bright yellow. (1-3 ft (30-90 cm)).

N. jurana, N. pumila subsp. *jurana*. This rare and diminutive species has tiny, yellow flowers no more than an inch (25 mm) across. It was once believed to be lost to cultivation, but is happily available once more. E. France. (1-1½ ft (30-45 cm)).

N. kalmiana Thought to be the American form of *N. pumila*, some authorities believe it to be closer to *N. rubrodisca* owing to its red, stigmatic disc. It has almost heart-shaped foliage and small, golden blossoms. North America. (1-1½ ft (30-45 cm)).

N. longifolia See *N. sagittifolia*.

N. lutea N. rivularis, Nenuphar luteum, Nymphaea lutea, Nymphozanthus luteus. Yellow Pond Lily, Brandy Bottle. The bottle-shaped yellow flowers emit an offensive alcoholic odour and are produced amongst masses of leathery, green, ovate, floating leaves. This species was of economic importance in northern Europe in years gone by: the rootstocks were powdered and made into bread by the Swedes, and when mixed with the membraneous inner layer of the bark of Scots pine, made an excellent cake. The rhizomes contain tannic acid, and have been used in tanning, for curing skin disorders and staunching bleeding wounds. The Greeks used to brew a potent cordial called pufer from the opened flowers. Europe including British Isles, N. Asia, rare in North Africa. (1-8 ft (30 cm-2 m 50 cm)).

N. lutea minima See *N. pumila.*

N. lutea var. *minor* See *N.* X *spennerana*.

N. lutea var. *pumila* See *N. pumila*.

N. lutea var. *punctata* The leaf surfaces are punctuated with small brown patches. (1-5 ft (30 cm-1 m 50 cm)).

N. lutea var. *purpureosignata* The yellow flowers have purple markings and stigmas. (1-5 ft (30 cm-1 m 50 cm)).

N. lutea var. *rubropetala* This bears yellow blooms with a red infusion. (1-5 ft (30 cm-1 m 50 cm)).

Figure 13.2
Nuphar lutea

N. lutea var. *sericea* This has large, intense-yellow flowers, and the petioles and leaf undersides are pubescent. Hungary. (1-5 ft (30 cm-1 m 50 cm)).

N. lutea var. *sericea denticulata* This is a form of the preceding, with slightly dentate foliage. (1-5 ft (30 cm-1 m 50 cm)).

N. lutea subsp. *ozarkana* See *N. ozarkana*.

N. lutea subsp. *variegata* See *N. variegata*.

N. macrophylla See *N. advena* var. *macrophylla*.

N. microphylla This is a delightful little plant with crispy, membraneous, underwater foliage and thin, olive-green, orbicular floating leaves with a distinct purplish cast. The bright-yellow flowers are less than an inch (25 mm) across. E. United States. (1-1½ ft (30-45 cm)).

N. microphylla f. *multisepala* This is a form which has been reported as occurring in the northern limits of its range, but is not yet in cultivation. (1-1½ ft (30-45 cm)).

N. minimum Dwarf Pond Lily, Least Yellow Pond Lily. There is tremendous confusion between this and *N. pumilum*, and many botanists now include the two under one or other name. Until they have been finally sorted out I have described both, as there are varieties allegedly derived from each species with those

Figure 13.3   *Nuphar microphylla* showing Portion of Plant with Submersed
and Floating Leaves x ½ (a), Flower x ½ (b), Fruit x ½ (c) and Seed x 3 (d);
N. rubrodisca showing Leaf x ½ (e), Flower x ½ (f), Fruit x ½ (g) and Seed
x 3 (h)

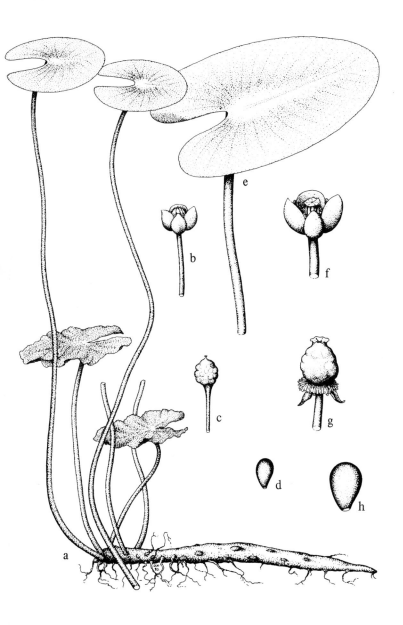

specific epithets appended; so in order to allay confusion, both names are given, although to the gardener the type plants appear to be the same. It is a splendid little plant for the shallows of a pool or in the sink garden or rockpool. The small, almost heart-shaped leaves have deeply cut basal sinuses, and the tiny blooms are yellow. N. and C. Europe, N. Asia. (1-1½ ft (30-45 cm)).

N. minimum var. *affinis N. pumilum* var. *affinis.* This is sometimes listed as an aquarium plant. It is possibly a geographical variation, producing pale-green leaves and small, yellow flowers, and is less robust than the type. C. Europe. (1 ft (30 cm)).

N. oguraensis Recorded as recently as 1934 from Honshu and Kyushu, Japan, this species has not been seen in general cultivation. The broad leaves, almost as wide as long, but seldom more than 3 in (8 cm) in length, have flattened petioles, and the flowers are scarcely 2 in (5 cm) across and yellow. (1-1½ ft (30-45 cm)).

N. orbiculata See *N. advena* var. *orbiculata*.

N. ozarkana, N. lutea subsp. *ozarkana*. This is a very similar species to *N. lutea* and was regarded by Beal in his revision of the genus as a subspecies of *N. lutea*. It differs principally in its rounded leaf tips and the oval shape of its petioles in cross-section. Its distribution is restricted to southern Missouri and Arkansas. (1-5 ft (30 cm-1 m 50 cm)).

N. polysepala Indian Pond Lily. This is an excellent plant for shallow water, although it is much larger in all its parts than either *N. lutea* or *N. advena*. The deep-green, broadly lanceolate foliage is up to a foot (30 cm) in length and almost as wide. The golden blossoms are occasionally tinged with red, and are up to 6 in (15 cm) across. N. America. (1-5 ft (30 cm-1 m 50 cm)).

N. pumilum, N. pumila, N. lutea var. *minima, Nymphaea lutea* var. *pumila*. Dwarf Pond Lily, Least Yellow Pond Lily. As far as the gardener is concerned this is the same as *N. minima*, although I would not care to say which name had precedence. The problem remains that while both species look superficially alike, they have varieties attributed to them which are clearly different. Until the botanists have resolved the confusion and decided upon a name, I have listed the plant under the two names by which it will be found in nurserymen's catalogues. The small, almost heart-shaped leaves have deeply cut, basal sinuses, and the tiny blooms are yellow. (1-1½ ft (30-45 cm)).

N. pumilum var. *affinis* See *N. minimum* var. *affinis*.

N. pumilum var. *ozeensis* This variety was reported from Honshu, Japan in 1951, but has not appeared in cultivation up to the present time. (1-1½ ft (30-45 cm)).

N. rivularis See *N. lutea*.

Figure 13.4   *Nuphar sagittifolia* showing Leaf x ¼ (a) and Fruit x ½ (b)
and *N. polysepala* showing Fruit x ½ (c), Leaf x ¼ (d) and Flower x ½ (e)

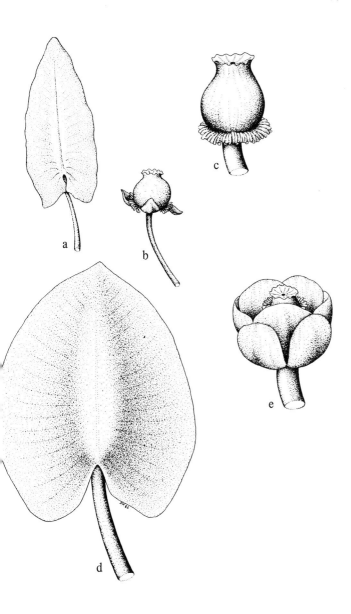

N. rubrodisca Red Disked Pond Lily. The large, yellow flowers have bright-crimson, central stigmatic discs. The handsome, crinkled, submerged foliage is long, floating or occasionally erect. It is believed by some authorities to be a natural hybrid. N. America. (1-3 ft (30-90 cm)).

N. sagittifolia, N. longifolia. Cape Fear Spatterdock. The soft-yellow flowers nestle amongst foliage that occasionally comes to the surface, and these are followed by curious, dull-green, marble-like fruits. Most of the leaves remain totally submerged, and are narrow, lanceolate and bright translucent green. Although once used in pools in the United States, *N. sagittifolia* quickly fell from favour, to be replaced by the *Nymphaeas*, and then became almost exclusively the prerogative of the aquarist. It makes an excellent centrepiece for the large cold-water aquarium. N. America. (1-5 ft (30 cm-1 m 50 cm)).

N. subintegerrima This Japanese species is not widely cultivated, and closely resembles *N. oguraensis*, except in the characteristics of the stigmatic disc. (1-1½ ft (30-45 cm)).

N. variegata, N. americana, N. advena var. *variegata, N. lutea* subsp. *variegata.* Greater Yellow Waterlily. Some authorities contend that this is a variety of *N. advena* owing to its similar distribution and the fact that it is virtually impossible to separate, except for the leaf sinus of *N. variegata* being narrower and often closed by the overlapping rounded lobes. The petioles are flattened on their upper surfaces with a narrow, flange-like extension down either side. This species always occurs growing in more acid conditions than *N. advena*. N. America. (1½-5 ft (45 cm-1 m 50 cm)).

Hybrids

N. japonica X *pumila* This recent, and as yet unnamed hybrid has received wide acclaim from aquarists. It produces the yellow blossoms of *N. japonica*, but possesses the attractive, translucent, underwater foliage of *N. pumila*. (1-1½ ft (30-45 cm)).

N. fletcheri (*N. advena* X *N. microphylla*?). Little is known of this plant except that it was recognised by Caspary, and was originally collected by a Mr Fletcher near Ottawa, Canada.

N. intermedia (*N. lutea* X *N. pumila*) A natural hybrid, this often appears in areas separate from those of its supposed parents. C. Europe and north to Lapland. (1-3 ft (30-90 cm)).

N. spennerana (*N.* X *intermedia* X *N. pumila*? *N. lutea* X *N. pumila*?). *N. lutea* var. *minor*. A very confusing plant, believed by most botanists to be a union between *N.* X *intermedia* and *N. pumila*, and by others to be a *N. lutea* and *N. pumila* cross. The small, yellow flowers have prominent, star-like ovaries, and the broad leaves are light green and translucent. N. and C. Europe including British Isles. (1-2 ft (30-60 cm)).

CHAPTER 14

Nelumbos

From time immemorial the sacred lotus or *Nelumbo* has been revered by man. In China the flower of the native *Nelumbo nucifera* has long been involved in religion as the seat of Buddha, and considered to be symbolic of female beauty; while in Egypt it is thought to have been the legendary Pythagorean bean, and has long been in cultivation there as a food crop. Almost all parts of the plant can be eaten: the long leaf stalks as salad, the thinly sliced rootstock roasted and eaten hot, or else iced and served with walnuts and apricots. They can also be salted down, and are said to preserve admirably if immersed in vinegar. The seeds, which are about the size of large peas, are also edible, with a taste like almonds.

Nelumbos are half-hardy aquatics with plate-like leaves held above the water on centrally placed petioles, which may be anything up to 8 ft (2 m 50 cm) high. The upper surfaces of the leaves are coated with a thin, waxy substance, so that when a drop of water falls onto them it runs about like quicksilver. The waterlily-like flowers are borne on long, slender stems which extend to just above the leaves, and are followed by curious seed heads which resemble the roses of small watering cans (Figure 14.1).

Cultivation is similar to that advocated for tropical waterlilies. The whitish, banana-like rootstocks come to hand during early spring, and should be planted in round tubs in a heavy loam compost enriched with a handful of coarse bonemeal (see also page 123). Plant horizontally about an inch (25 mm) beneath the soil, and then add 2 or 3 in (5 or 8 cm) of water. As the young foliage emerges, gradually raise the level of the water until it is about 9 in (23 cm) deep. Routine summer care is confined to watching for aphids and supporting any foliage that becomes top heavy. As autumn approaches, the water is slowly drained away so that the foliage dies down. The roots may then be lifted, washed, and stored in boxes of damp sand in a frost-free place for the winter.

Propagation is usually effected by breaking off the tubers at points where they narrow, ensuring that each portion has a terminal shoot, and then planting in the normal manner. The species, however, are also readily propagated by seeds, which are sown singly in pots of heavy loam and placed in an aquarium which is kept at a temperature of 75°-80°F (23°-27°C). The juvenile leaves will float on the surface, but as the plants grow stronger they are thrust above in typical fashion. Pot on as and when necessary in the same heavy loam, but with a sprinkling of coarse bonemeal added. After two seasons they can be expected to run into flower.

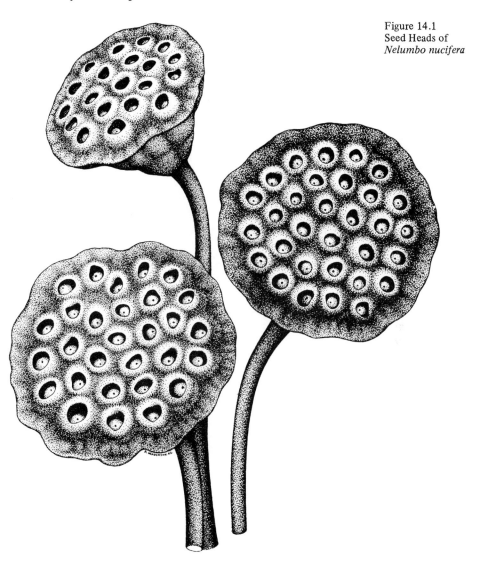

Figure 14.1
Seed Heads of
Nelumbo nucifera

Species and their Varieties

Nelumbo alba var. *floribunda* See *N. nucifera* var. *alba grandiflora*.

N. lutea See *N. pentapetala*.

N. nucifera, *N. speciosa*, *Nelumbium speciosum*, *Nelumbium indicum*, *Nelumbium nelumbo*, *Nymphaea nelumbo*. East Indian Lotus, Sacred Lotus. The immense blooms up to a foot (30 cm) across change from vivid rose to flesh-pink with age. The large rounded leaves are on petioles 6 or 7 ft (1 m 85 cm-2 m 15 cm) high. Philippine, India, N. Australia, Japan.

Figure 14.2
Nelumbo nucifera

N. nucifera var. *alba Nelumbium speciosum* var. *album*. Magnolia Lotus. This is a pure-white form of the type.

N. nucifera var. *alba grandiflora*, *N. alba* var. *floribunda*, *Nelumbium speciosum* var. *album grandiflorum*. The immense, fragrant, ivory goblets in excess of a foot (30 cm) across, with a central boss of golden stamens, are held high above large, pea-green foliage.

N. nucifera var. *alba plena*, *Nelumbium speciosum* var. *album plenum*, *N.* 'Shiroman'. This is a Japanese selection, with large, fragrant double, creamy-white flowers intensifying to pure white with age.

N. nucifera var. *alba striata*, *N.* 'Empress' *Nelumbium speciosum album* 'Striatum'. The very fragrant, pure-white blooms are tipped and streaked with crimson.

N. nucifera var. *albo-virens*, *Nelumbium speciosum* var. *album virens*. The rounded, double, white flowers are flushed and stained with green when young, but clear to pure white with age. It was introduced by Sturtevant in 1907.

N. nucifera var. *gigantea*, *Nelumbium speciosum* var. *gigantea*. The enormous, purplish-rose flowers are set amidst immense, pea-green leaves with silvery reverses.

N. nucifera var. *rosea*, *Nelumbium speciosum* var. *roseum*, *N.* 'Dawn'. The large flowers are a delicate pale pink.

N. nucifera var. *rosea plena*, *N.* 'Double Dawn', *Nelumbium speciosum* var. *roseum plenum*. This is the much deeper-coloured, double form.

Note: Many of the above forms of *N. nucifera*, although attributed to natural variations of the species, have been in cultivation for many years, and their origins have been lost in the mists of time. It is possible that some are early selections. The cultivar names attributed to some of these forms are of recent origin and are the invention of nurserymen, although some are generally accepted in the trade. The following are cultivar names used by nurserymen for selections from *N. nucifera*.

'Dawn' See *N. nucifera* var. *rosea*.
'Double Dawn' See *N. nucifera* var. *rosea plena*.
'Empress' See *N. nucifera* var. *alba striata*.
'Shiroman' See *N. nucifera* var. *alba plena*.

N. pentapetala, *N. lutea*, *Nelumbium luteum*, *Nymphaea pentapetala*. American Lotus, Duck Acorn, Water Chinkapin, Pondnuts, Wonkapin. The large leaves, 2 ft (60 cm) across are borne on stems up to 3 ft (90 cm) high. The flowers are 8 in (20 cm) across and of a uniform shade of pale sulphur. It does not flower freely until well established, but buds are initiated at a lower temperature than in *N. nucifera*. 1810. North America, Central America, West Indies, Colombia.

N. pentapetala var. *flavescens*, *N.* 'Flavescens'. *Nelumbium luteum* var. *flavescens*. This is a smaller-flowered variety, but with a conspicuous red spot at the base of each petal and in the centre of each leaf. It was introduced by Marliac as a variety of *N. pentapetala*, but it may well be a hybrid.

Hybrids

The following are believed to have been derived by hybridisation or as further selections from deliberate crosses. In most cases their

Figure 14.3   *Nelumbo pentapetala* showing Part of a Plant with Creeping Rootstock x ⅙ (a), Flower x ¼ (b), Flower bud x ¼ (c), Receptacle with Imbedded Carpels x ¼ (d), Vertical Section of Receptacle x ½ (e), Seed x 1 (f) and Petal x ½ (g)

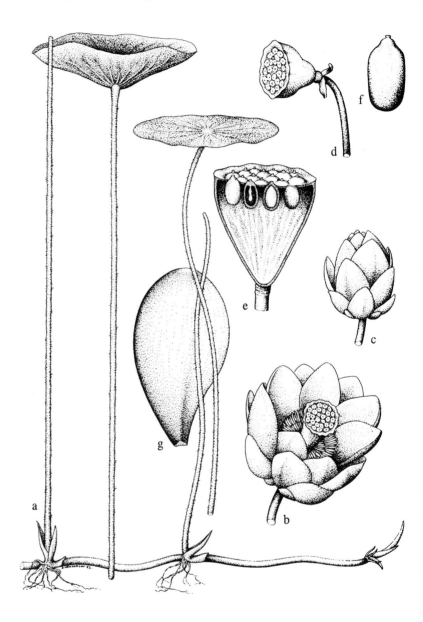

parentage is unknown, most having been in cultivation for many years.

'Chaw An Basu' This is the name given by the Japanese to 'Momo Botan' and means 'Rice Bowl Lotus'. The cultivar 'Chawan Basu' is an entirely different plant.

'Chawan Basu' This is a semi-dwarf, free-flowering variety with beautiful white blossoms edged with pink, and it will grow well in a confined space.

'Grossherzog Ernst Ludwig' (*N. pentapetala* var. *flavescens* X *N.* 'Osiris'.) The exotic blooms look like rosy-red brandy glasses, and have golden stamens and conspicuous green ovaries. The handsome foliage is sea-green.

'Japonica Rosea' The large, double flowers are flushed and overlaid with rose. The foliage is glaucous.

'Kermesina' This very fine, double, red variety is of Japanese origin.

'Kinshiren' The medium-sized, white blooms are flushed with soft rose-pink.

'Lily Pons' This bears large, salmon-pink, cup-shaped flowers.

'Madame Paufique' The flowers are white, flushed with carmine.

'Mrs Perry D. Slocum' (*N. pentapetala* X *N. nucifera* var. *rosea plena*). This is the most spectacular lotus of all. The massive blossoms, up to a foot (30 cm) across, are fully double and open rose-pink, but pass to creamy-yellow with each succeeding day. Raised by Perry Slocum on his former nursery at Binghamton, it was introduced in 1965. It requires plenty of room as it will grow at least 5 or 6 ft (1 m 50 cm-1 m 85 cm) high.

'Momo Botan', 'Chaw an Basu'. This bears fully double, carmine blossoms on small plants, and it is of similar habit to the Pygmaea types, but with much larger flowers. It can be grown successfully in quite a small tub.

'Osiris' This hybrid, probably the most popular of them all, has huge, globular, rose-pink blooms and bluish-green foliage.

'Pekinensis Rubra' The intense dark-crimson flowers are of a thick, velvety texture, and it is very fragrant.

'Pekinensis Rubra Plena' This is a much less floriferous, double form.

'Pulchra' The lavender-rose blooms are streaked and lined with red.

'Pygmaea Alba' This miniature form has leaves no more than a foot (30 cm) high and 6 in (15 cm) across. The pure-white flowers are some 4 in (10 cm) in diameter.

'Pygmaea Alba Plena' This is a double form of the above.

'Pygmaea Rosea' The tiny, single flowers are an intense rose-pink.

'Violacea' The deep, plum-red flowers are lightly streaked and veined with white. It is a shy bloomer.

CHAPTER 15

Victoria and Euryale

The giant *Victoria* waterlily was first discovered in South America by Haenke in 1801, but his discovery was not made known until 1848. Bonpland came across it in 1820, but it was not until 1832 that Poeppigg eventually described it as *Euryale amazonica*. Schomburgk came across the *Victoria* in the Berbice river in Guyana in 1837, and recorded the association between the blossoms and a pollinating beetle. About this time much more information came to light, and the plant was re-named *Victoria amazonica* in honour of the reigning monarch. Seed was sent regularly by Bridges from Bolivia to Kew in the early 1840s, but it was not until 1849 that the raising of *Victoria* plants was mastered, and seedlings were distributed to a number of major gardens. One recipient was Paxton, gardener to the Duke of Devonshire at Chatsworth, who in November 1849 was the first person to flower the plant under cultivation. Amongst much excitement a flower and leaf were presented to Queen Victoria. In later years the remarkable structure of the leaf of the *Victoria* inspired Paxton to design a new conservatory based upon its characteristics, a design that was used for the ill-fated Crystal Palace.

Of course the cultivation of *Victoria* in temperate regions is the prerogative of parks and botanical gardens where plenty of room is available, but in warmer climes where it can be grown outside it is a plant of great beauty and merit that can be accommodated in any sizeable pool. The seeds are about the size of a pea, and ripen during late autumn and early winter. They are stored in water or saturated, green sphagnum moss in a test tube until required for sowing during early spring. They are then sown individually in small pots in a compost that is roughly equivalent to John Innes Compost, but devoid of the base fertiliser, which tends to pollute the water. A generous mixture of dried blood and bonemeal is a suitable substitute. A thin layer of clean silver sand is then spread over the surface of the compost, and the pots are submerged in water maintained at a temperature of 75°F (23°C). After three weeks or so the seeds germinate and push up two or three small hastate leaves, which lie

142

just under the surface of the water. The fourth and fifth leaves usually prove to be the first floating leaves and are some 6 or 8 in (15 or 20 cm) in diameter. At this stage the plant should be re-potted into an 8 or 10 in (20 or 25 cm) pot, and stood in the pool in about 18 in (45 cm) of water.

Figure 15.1
Girl on a *Victoria* Leaf

During the next month round, juvenile floating leaves will be produced regularly at the rate of two or three a week, gradually increasing in size until reaching some 2 ft (60 cm) across, when the characteristic upturned edge will be evident. This is the true adult floating leaf, and its production indicates that the plant is ready for re-potting. As the *Victoria* is a gross feeder, the new compost should be considerably enriched with well-rotted animal manure, and the plant potted in a container of ample dimensions and replaced in the water with the water level raised a further 6 or 9 in (15 or 23 cm). After a few days the searching roots penetrate the manure and a great surge of growth takes place. New leaves are produced, rapidly increasing in size until they are upwards of 6 ft (1 m 85 cm) across, with an upturned edge 6 to 9 in (15 to 23 cm) high. It is about this time that the first flowers are produced.

Few people have seen the expanded blooms in their full glory, for they are nocturnal and short-lived, lasting but two nights. Each flower is a very complex structure some 12 in (30 cm) in diameter and containing myriad petals. When the young buds burst the emerging petals are pure white, but turn to an agreeable shade of pale pink by early the first morning. The following night the pale-pink flower opens amidst a delicious pineapple fragrance which increases in intensity as the night wears on, until the ageing flower, which by this time is a deep plum colour, slowly disintegrates.

143

Pollination of the blossoms under natural conditions is by water beetles which become trapped amongst the petals as they close after the first night. Obviously, under glass artificial pollination must take place if a good seed crop is to result.

The Species
and Varieties

Victoria amazonica, V. regia, V. regia var. *randii, Euryale amazonica.*
Royal Waterlily, Water Platter, Yrupe. This is the original Victoria as cultivated by Paxton, but at present it would appear that *V. cruziana* enjoys wider popularity. The sepals of *V. amazonica* are prickly right to the tips, and the undersides of the leaves deep red and scarcely pubescent. Amazon, Guyana.

V. cruziana, V. trikeri. Santa Cruz Waterlily. This is the species currently encountered more often in cultivation. The sepals are only prickly at their base and the leaves densely villous and blue-green beneath. It enjoys a more southerly distribution, occurring from Paraguay and Bolivia to Argentina.

V. 'Longwood Hybrid' (*V. amazonica* X *V. cruziana*). This little-cultivated hybrid was raised at Longwood Gardens, Pennsylvania, in 1961.

V. regia See *V. amazonica.*

V. regia var. *randii* See *V. amazonica.*

V. trikeri See *V. cruziana.*

The *Euryale* is very closely related to the *Victoria*, differing principally in the size of foliage and lack of an upturned edge on adult leaves. Although little cultivated, it is worth considering, for it is of similar habit to *Victoria*, but of more modest dimensions. Cultivation is exactly the same as that afforded to *Victoria*.

Euryale amazonica See *V. amazonica.*

E. ferox The lone species, introduced to Europe in 1809 by Roxburgh, Director of the Calcutta Botanic Garden, it has flat, circular leaves up to 4 ft (1 m 20 cm) across with spiny undersides. The flowers are up to 4 in (10 cm) in diameter, deep violet, and followed by farinaceous seeds like small nuts. India, China, Bangladesh.

CHAPTER 16

Pests and Diseases

Waterlilies are attacked by a number of pests and diseases. Fortunately, those that are specific to members of the Nymphaeaceae are few and far between, but they can nevertheless be very difficult to control, particularly when there are fish in the pool. The merest trace of an insecticide or fungicide in the water will cause fatalities.

Waterlily Aphis

Pests

A number of species of aphis attack waterlilies, but it is the waterlily aphid, *Rhopalosiphum nymphaeae*, that is the most troublesome. In warm, humid weather it breeds at a prodigious rate, smothering all exposed parts of the plants and causing widespread disfigurement. Although lavishing its attention upon *Nymphaeas*, *Nuphars* and other allied genera, it will also attack succulent aquatics such as *Menyanthes* and *Sagittaria*.

The late summer brood of adults lay eggs on the boughs of plum and cherry trees during early autumn. These overwinter and hatch during the following spring, giving rise to winged females which fly to the waterlilies. Here they reproduce asexually and give birth to live, wingless females which continue the process every few days. With the approach of autumn, winged males and females are produced. These unite sexually and the females deposit their eggs on the overwintering host.

When infested plants are in a pool without livestock, a contact wash such as pyrethrum or nicotine soap can be used to effect a control. However, when fish are present little can be done other than to forcibly spray the foliage with a jet of clear water in order to dislodge the pests, which will then be readily devoured by the goldfish. As with most problems of this nature, prevention is better than cure. Therefore, the eliminating or reducing of overwintering populations by spraying all nearby plum and cherry trees with DNOC Tar Oil Wash during the winter months is to be recommended.

Waterlily Beetle

The waterlily beetle, *Galerucella nymphaeae*, although of only local occurrence, is probably the most destructive of all waterlily pests. The small and shiny-black larvae are usually seen scrambling about the foliage or amongst the petals of open flowers. They devour any succulent part of the waterlily with equal indifference, stripping away the epidermal tissue of both flower and foliage, leaving the tattered remains to decay. The adult beetles do not appear to be so destructive, and can often be observed feeding on either pollen or nectar, often unwittingly pollinating the blossom at the same time.

During the winter the beetles hibernate in pool-side vegetation, migrating to the waterlilies towards the end of May or early June. Here they deposit their eggs in clusters on the upper surfaces of the leaves, between six and twelve at a time, at intervals of two or three days. Each female has definite egg-laying periods that last from ten to twenty days. During this time up to a hundred eggs may be deposited by one beetle. When newly laid the eggs are a golden-yellow, but quickly change to white.

After a week or so they hatch out into curious black larvae with distinctive yellow bellies, a black head, and three pairs of black legs. These are quite tiny — less than half-an-inch (15 mm) long — but nevertheless have voraceous appetites, and can be observed feeding both day and night. When they first emerge they are easily spotted, for they cluster together in irregular formation, but after a day or two disperse.

Pupation takes place both on waterlilies and on the foliage of nearby aquatic plants. The pupae are black, of similar size and shape to the larvae, and take up to two weeks to metamorphose. Under favourable conditions three, or sometimes four, generations will be produced in a season. In the presence of fish little can be done apart from spraying the plants with clear water and dislodging the pests. However, in the absence of livestock malathion provides an effective control. But either way, one of the most successful means of reducing infestation is to remove and burn all dead and dying pool-side vegetation in the early autumn in order to deprive the beetles of winter protection.

China Mark Moths

There are two species of china mark moths which prey upon *Nymphaeas* and *Nuphars*: the beautiful china mark moth, *Nymphula stagnata*, and the brown china mark moth, *N. nympheata*. However, it is the latter that is most frequently encountered.

The larva of this comparatively insignificant brown and orange moth can be a real menace, for not only does it cut and shred the foliage of waterlilies and other succulent aquatic plants, but also prior to pupation makes a shelter for itself by sticking down two pieces of leaf in which it then weaves a greyish, silky cocoon.

Eggs are laid during late summer in neat rows along the undersides of floating foliage. They hatch in about two weeks, and the tiny caterpillars burrow into the undersides of the foliage and later make small oval cases out of the leaves. Feeding continues until the winter, when they seem to disappear. Unfortunately, they re-appear as the spring sunshine warms the water, continue feeding, and ultimately weave their silky cocoons.

The beautiful china mark moth has similar habits, except that the caterpillars burrow into the petioles or leaf stems during the early stages of their lives. In due course they hibernate there, but later emerge to make characteristic leaf cases and subsequently white, silky cocoons.

Small infestations of either species can be hand-picked, care being taken to collect all leafy debris floating on the water, as this may also have cocoons attached. When damage is widespread it is preferable to remove all floating foliage and debris and destroy it, allowing the juvenile submerged leaves to take over, thereby giving the plant a completely fresh start. Chemical control is generally ineffective as the caterpillars and cocoons are protected by their leafy shelters.

Caddis Flies

The majority of the 185 native British species of caddis fly produce larvae which feed upon the foliage of aquatic plants. A number are totally aquatic in their larval stage and swim around the pool with little shelters made of shells, sand, sticks and pieces of plant surrounding them. All belong to the order Trichoptera, and the species *Limnephilus marmoratus* and *Halesus radiatus* are particularly common.

Adult flies visit the pool in the cool of the evening, depositing up to a hundred eggs at a time in a mass of jelly which swells up as soon as it touches the water. This is often hooked around submerged foliage in a long cylindrical string, or attached to the aerial foliage of reeds or rushes and allowed to trail in the water.

Within ten days or a fortnight the larvae emerge and immediately start spinning their silky cases and collecting material with which to construct their shelters. At this stage they feed not only on waterlilies, but any aquatic plants, devouring leaves, stems, flowers and roots. Eventually they pupate, usually on the floor of the pool, emerging as dull, moth-like insects with brown or greyish wings.

Once again chemical control is difficult, as the larvae are protected by their shelters. However, an adequate stock of fish will keep the population within bounds, as fish consider the succulent larvae a great delicacy.

False Leaf-mining Midge

The minute larvae of the false leaf-mining midge, *Cricotopus ornatus*, sometimes attack the foliage of *Nymphaeas* and *Nuphars*, creating a narrow tracery of lines over the surface of the leaves which then turn brown and decay. Nicotine or malathion can be used in the absence of livestock, but a forcible jet of clear water is all that can be recommended when fish are present.

Snails

Although snails are often suggested as useful additions to the garden pool, only the ramshorn, *Planorbis corneus*, can be unreservedly recommended. This is a species with a somewhat flattened shell like a catherine wheel, which the creature carries in an upright position on its back. It feeds almost exclusively on algae and is thus very useful in maintaining a balance within the pool. This is in contrast to its often recommended cousin, the great pond snail or freshwater whelk, *Limnaea stagnalis*. While it may be argued that it is perfectly suitable for large expanses of water, great pond snails only bring trouble when introduced to the average-sized garden pool. Apart from the unfortunate fact that it is an intermediary host for a fish disease passed in a circle by the seagull via the snail to the fish, it has an infuriating habit of ignoring algae in the pond, and turning its attention to waterlily pads and broad-leafed oxygenating plants, reducing them to nothing more than tattered scraps of vegetation.

L. stagnalis is an easily recognisable species with a tall, spiralled and pointed shell an inch or two (25mm - 5cm) high, and a fleshy, greyish-cream body. It lays its eggs in the same manner as *Planorbis*, but instead of enclosing them in flat pads of jelly, they are laid in distinctive, long, gelatinous cylinders which are readily detected on the undersides of waterlily leaves. If *Limnaea* snails have entered the pool by accident, either on the plants or by some other means, then they can be captured quite quickly by floating a lettuce leaf or old cabbage stalk on the surface of the water. After twenty-four hours the leaf or stalk will be smothered in hungry snails and can be removed and destroyed.

The fountain bladder snail, *Physa fontinalis*, is another undesirable character, much like a very tiny whelk with a short, fleshy body and slender feelers. It is a particular nuisance in the smaller pool, puncturing the leaves of waterlilies and gnawing at the edges until eventually they crumble and disintegrate. Although they are seldom introduced deliberately, most pools have a complement of these creatures. In small volumes of water they should be captured and destroyed as outlined earlier before they defoliate all the floating leaf plant population.

Bobitis nelumbialis

This insect pest has no common name and is specific to *Nelumbos*. It is recognisable as a small grub which has rolled and gummed itself between the edges of young leaves, which it then feeds on in comparative safety. Hand-picking is the only control, although spraying with a systemic insecticide can be advocated in the absence of fish.

Waterlily Leaf Spots

Two leaf-spot diseases commonly affect waterlilies in this country. The most common is *Ovularia nymphaerum*, which causes dark patches to appear on the foliage. These rot through and cause the eventual disintegration of the leaves. It is particularly troublesome in a wet summer and as soon as detected, affected leaves should be removed and burnt.

Various *Cercosporae* species cause the other kind of leaf spot, and although not quite so common are equally destructive. Affected foliage becomes brown and dry at the edges, eventually crumbling and wasting away. Removing and destroying diseased leaves is the only effective cure, although a weak solution of Bordeaux mixture sprayed over the foliage will help check the spread of the disease.

Fasciation

For some reason waterlilies, more than any other decorative garden plants, seem prone to fasciation. This is the condition which usually appertains when cells on one side of the plant increase at a faster rate than their counterparts, and grotesque flattened and distorted leaf and flower stems result. Flowers and foliage are also contorted and may be produced in large quantities. In the case of blossoms, multi-heading is common, but many of the individual blooms thus formed are incomplete or badly twisted.

The reasons for fasciation in *Nymphaeas* are not clearly understood, and while in a number of cases it is thought to be a physiological disorder, there is abundant evidence to support the theory that a bacterial disease is in large measure responsible. How infectious this may be is difficult to ascertain, for its effect upon waterlilies cannot be said to be widespread, for the present at least. As normal 'eyes' removed from a disease-fasciated plant usually grow into normal plants, it would seem unnecessary to contemplate anything so drastic as pool sterilisation. Removal and destruction of contorted plants would appear to be the only remedy necessary.

Glossary

Anther	The part of the stamen containing the pollen grain.
Calyx	The sepals as a whole.
Dehisce	Burst open to shed seeds.
Form (f.)	(Forma) Botanical classification below variety.
Genus	Group of species with common characteristics.
Glaucous	Bluish-green bloom.
Globose	Globular or rounded.
Hybrid	Plant produced by fertilisation of one species by another.
Lanceolate	Narrow, tapering at each end.
Obovate	Egg-shaped, but with narrow end at the base.
Obovoid	Solidly obovate.
Orbicular	Rounded, with length and breadth about the same.
Ovate	Egg-shaped.
Ovoid	Egg-shaped (of a solid object).
Peduncle	The stalk of a flower.
Peltate	With the stalk attached to the centre (of a leaf).
Petaloid	Brightly coloured and resembling petals.
Petiole	Leaf stalk.
pH	The acid/alkaline status of a soil, etc. A neutral condition is taken as pH 7.0, all figures lower than this denoting degrees of acidity; those above, alkalinity.
Pistil	Female reproductive organ in a flowering plant.
Pubescent	Covered with fine, short hairs.
Rhizome	An underground stem lasting more than one season.
Sagittate	Arrow-shaped.
Sepal	Outer part of a flower which is usually green and leaf-like.
Sinus	Depression between two lobes or teeth.
Spathulate	Paddle-shaped.
Species	The specific plant within a genus.
Stamens	Male reproductive organs in a flowering plant.

Stellate	Star-shaped.
Stigma	The top of the pistil.
Style	The part connecting the ovary with the stigma.
Subspecies	Botanical classification below species.
Tuber	Swollen portion of stem or root of one year's duration.
Villous	Covered with shaggy hairs.
Viviparous	Producing young plants vegetatively.

Appendix I

The species of the genera *Nymphaea, Nuphar, Nelumbo, Victoria* and *Euryale* together with their authorities:

THE GENUS NYMPHAEA

Nymphaea alba (L.) Presl.
N.amazonum Martius and
    Zuccarini
N.ambla (Salisb.) DC
N.blanda G.F.W. Meyer
N.burttii Pring and Woodson
N.calliantha Conard
N.candida Presl.
N.capensis Thunb.
N.coerulea Savigny
N.colorata Peter
N.divaricata Hutchinson
N.elegans (Hook.)
N.fennica Mela.
N.flavo-virens Lehmann
N.gardneriana Planchon
N.gibertii (Morong.)
N.gigantea Hook
N.heudelotii Planchon
N.jamesoniana Planchon
N.lasiophylla Martius and
    Zuccarini

N.lotus (L.) Willdenow
N.mexicana Zuccarini
N.micrantha Guiller and Perrott
N.nitida Sims
N.nubica Lehmann
N.odorata Aiton
N.ovalifolia Conard
N.oxypetala Planchon
N.polychroma Peter
N.pubescens Willdenow
N.rubra Roxb.
N.rudgeana G.F.W. Meyer
N.stellata Willdenow
N.stenaspidota Caspary
N.stuhlmannii Schwfth. and
    Gilg.
N.sulfurea Gilg.
N.tenuinervia Caspary
N.tetragona Georgi
N.tuberosa Paine
N.zenkeri Gilg.

THE GENUS NUPHAR

Nuphar advena Aiton
N.fraterna (Mill. and Standl.)
    Standl.
N.japonica DC.
N.jurana

N.kalmiana Hook.
N.lutea (L.) Sm.
N.microphylla (Pers.) Fernald.
N.minimum Spenner
N.oguraensis Miki.

N.ozarkana (Mill. and Standl.)
  Standl.
N.polysepala Engelm.
N.pumilum (Timm) Decandolle

N.rubrodisca Morong.
N.sagittifolia (Walt.) Pursh.
N.subintegerrima (Casa) Makino
N.variegata Engelm.

THE GENUS NELUMBO

Nelumbo nucifera Gaertn.

N.pentapetala Fern.

THE GENUS VICTORIA

Victoria amazonica Sowerby

V.cruziana Orbigny

THE GENUS EURYALE

Euryale ferox Salisb.

Appendix II

Rectangular Pools (or Aquaria)

Multiply length (l) by width (w) by depth ($de.$) in feet to obtain volume in cubic feet. Multiply this by 6.25 to give the capacity in gallons.

$$(\text{vol.} = l \times w \times de. \; ; \; \text{cap.} = \text{vol.} \times 6.25 \text{ gal})$$

Circular Pools

Multiply depth ($de.$) in feet by the square of the diameter (d^2) in feet by 4.9 to give approximate gallonage.

$$(\text{cap.} = de. \times d^2 \times 4.9 \text{ gal})$$

Capacity of rectangular pools one foot average depth in **Gallons** (Imperial)

Breadth (ft)	Length (ft)						
	2	4	6	8	10	12	16
2	25	50	75	100	125	150	200
3	38	75	112	150	186	275	300
4	50	100	150	200	250	300	400
5	62	125	186	250	310	375	500
6	75	150	225	300	375	450	600

Capacity of circular garden pools in **Gallons** (Imperial)

Diameter (ft)	Average Depth of Water in inches				
	12	18	24	30	36
4	78	117	156	195	234
6	176	264	352	440	528
8	313	470	626	783	939
10	489	734	978	1223	1467
12	705	1058	1410	1763	2115

One Imperial gallon of water occupies 0.16 cubic feet, and weighs 10lb.

One US gallon is equivalent to 0.83268 Imperial gallon or 3.785 litres, and weighs 8.3lb.

One cubic foot of water is equivalent to 6.24 Imperial gallons or 28.3 litres, and weighs 62.32lb.

One Imperial gallon equals 160 fluid ounces or 4.546 litres.

One litre equals 1.76 Imperial pints or 0.22 Imperial gallons or 35.196 fluid ounces.

One litre equals 0.264 US gallons.

Great Britain

Bennetts Waterlily Farm,
Chickerell,
Weymouth,
Dorset.

J. and F. Mimmack,
Woodholme Nursery,
Goatsmoor Lane,
Stock,
Essex.

Jackamoors Hardy Plant Farm,
Theobalds Park Road,
Enfield,
Middlesex.

Lotus Water Garden Products Ltd,
Chesham,
Bucks.

P. and A. Plant Supplies Ltd,
The Nursery,
Sutton,
Norfolk

Stapeley Water Gardens Ltd,
Stapeley,
Nantwich,
Cheshire CW5 7JL.

Wildwoods Water Garden Centre,
Theobalds Park Road,
Enfield,
Middlesex.

France

Establishments Latour Marliac,
31 Allees De Tourny,
Bordeaux,
France.

R. Bezançon,
15 Avenue Du Raincy,
94 Saint Maur,
France.

New Zealand

Liliponds,
Murray L. Williams,
Eskdale RD2,
Napier,
New Zealand.

Italy

Giardini Di Marignolle,
Via Di Marignolle, 69,
50124. Firenze.

USA

Slocum Water Gardens,
1101 Cypress Gardens Road,
Winter Haven,
Florida. 33880.

Van Ness Water Gardens,
2460 North Euclid Avenue,
Upland,
California. 91786.

William Tricker Inc.
74 Allendale Avenue,
P.O. Box 398,
Saddle River,
NJ 07458.

Submerged
Oxygenating
Plants

Elodea canadensis. Water Thyme. Canadian Pondweed. Despite its reputation for being invasive this is one of the most useful submerged oxygenating plants. Dark green serrulate or curved lance-like leaves borne in whorls around long branching stems. Tiny floating lilac flowers with trailing thread-like stalks.

Fontinalis antipyretica. Willow Moss. A fairly dwarf growing plant with thick tangled dark green mossy foliage. Prefers acid water and by its very character is a perfect spawning plant for fish.

Hottonia palustris. Water Violet. Handsome whorled pale green foliage and spikes of lilac or white flowers held above the surface of the water during early summer. A North American relative, *H. inflata*, is very similar but with inflated branched flower stems.

Lagarosiphon major. Formerly known as *Elodea crispa* and very popular amongst pet dealers for the goldfish bowl trade. Long succulent snake-like stems densely clothed in broad dark green crispy foliage.

Myriophyllum spicatum. Milfoil. Long trailing stems which support spiked dense whorls of narrow submerged leaves and spikes of small reddish or greenish flowers.

Potomogeton crispus. Curled Pondweed. Handsome serrated and undulating bronze-green translucent leaves. Small but significant deep crimson and cream flowers on short stout spikes held above the surface of the water.

Index

Adelaide Botanic Gardens 49
Algae control 118

Bahnson, Dr Henry 28
Bisset, Peter 88
Bobitis nelumbialis 149
Bonpland 142
Burtt, B. 58

Caddis flies 147
Calcutta Botanic Garden 144
Cambridge Botanic Gardens, Mass.
  56
Chatsworth 142
China mark moths 146
Chou Tun-I 13
Conard 11, 71
Cricotopus ornatus 148

Euryale: propagation 142, 143, 144;
  routine care 142, 143, 144

False leaf-mining midge 148
Fasciation 149
Froebel, Otto 41

Galerucella nymphaeae 146

Haenke 142
Halesus radiatus 147
Harvey, E.T. 88
Hentze 23

Kew 48, 142

Latour-Marliac, Joseph Bory 11, 14,
  23, 43, 45, 87
Laydeker, Maurice 43
Limnaea stagnalis 148
Limnephilus marmoratus 147
Longwood Gardens 81, 144

Miller, Phillip 13
Millspaugh 27
Missouri Botanical Gardens 31, 58,
82. 87, 88

Nelumbo: planting 136; propagation
  136, 137; routine care 136
Nuphar, routine care 127
Nymphula nympheata 146
N. stagnata 146

Ovularia nymphaerum 149

Paxton 14, 142, 144
Perry, Amos 87
Perry, Frances 87
Physa fontinalis 148
Planorbis corneus 148
Poeppigy 142
Pollination 89
Pool: concrete 107; design 102;
  liners 103; natural 116; pre-
  shaped 105; rock 105, 107
Pring, George 14, 31, 58, 71, 82, 87-91
Propagation: eyes 121; plantlets 125;
  seed 120

Randig, Martin 89
Rhopalosiphum nymphaeae 145
Richardson, George 41
Roxburgh 144

Sagot 66
Schomburgk 142
Seed collection 90
Slocum, Perry 89, 141
Snails 148
Sturtevant, E.D. 48

Trickeri 71
Tub culture 123

Victoria: propagation 142; routine
  care 142, 143, 144

Waterlilies (Hardy): for cutting 22;
  feeding 116; planting 112; routine
  care 116, 119

Waterlilies (Tropical): planting 123; routine care 124; storage 124
Waterlily: aphis 145; baskets 110; beetle 146; compost 110; leaf spots 149
Wolff, Stephen 88